SANDRO
BOTTICELLI

Houghton.

HEAD OF THE MADONNA OF THE POMEGRANATE (UFFIZI).

SANDRO BOTTICELLI

BY JULIA CARTWRIGHT

(MRS. ADY)

DESORMAIS

LONDON

DUCKWORTH & CO.

HENRIETTA ST. COVENT GARDEN

" *Finally, good painting is a music and melody which intellect only can appreciate, and that with great difficulty. This painting is so rare that few are capable of attaining to it.*"

MICHELANGELO

Published 1903
Reissued 1914

PRINTED AT
THE BALLANTYNE PRESS
LONDON

CONTENTS

5

LIST OF PHOTOGRAVURES

LIST OF PHOTOGRAVURES

8

I

1444—1475

ALESSANDRO DEI FILIPEPI, or Sandro Botticelli as he was familiarly called by his contemporaries, is one of the most interesting among the Florentine painters of the Renaissance. Both his art and personality have had a singular fascination for the scholars and critics of the nineteenth century. The strong individuality of his conceptions, the depth and originality of his thought, his fine poetic imagination and keen sense of beauty, appeal in a peculiar manner to the modern mind, and have made him as popular in the present day as he was in his own lifetime. The great thinkers of the last generation who first opened our eyes to the forgotten glories of the early Renaissance, and the experts who have brought the scientific methods of the new criticism to bear upon these questions, agree in their admiration for this rare master. Ruskin and Pater have enshrined Botticelli's name in immortal prose ; Morelli and Mr. Berenson have pronounced him to be " a creative and original genius of the first rank," as well as " the greatest lineal designer that Europe has ever had."

Above all, we have in Botticelli a typical Florentine artist, who gave expression to the life and thought of his fellow-citizens more fully than any master of the age. The other great painters who flourished towards the close of the fifteenth century were soon drawn away from the city of their birth. Leonardo spent the best years of his life at Milan and went to die in France ; Michelangelo belongs more to Rome than he does to Florence, and his most famous paintings are to be seen in the Vatican chapel. But Sandro spent almost the whole of his life in Florence and is closely associated with her greatest age and the golden days when Giovanni Rucellai thanked God that he had been allowed to live.

Born in the time of Cosimo, the father of his country, Botticelli became the favourite painter of that great citizen's still more illustrious grandson, Lorenzo dei Medici, who employed him to record the triumph of his house and the ruin of his foes on the walls of Florence. An intimate friend and companion of the humanists, whom the Magnifico delighted to honour, he painted the classical myths of the Greek world with which they were enamoured, as it appeared in their eyes. His Venus and Pallas, his nymphs and Cupids, were inspired by their verses. Every detail of the Primavera or the Villa Lemmi frescoes was supplied by Angelo Poliziano or Marsilio Ficino. Their enthusiasm for antiquity, their love of natural beauty, even their revived interest in Dante are all reflected in Botticelli's works. The same Christian idealism which made Pico and Ficino seek to reconcile the doctrine of Plato with the faith of Christ, moved Sandro to paint those Madonnas in which the deepest human tenderness and the purest religious feeling is combined with the highest decorative beauty. And this same mystic tendency led Botticelli to listen to the great Dominican preacher whose voice had so strange an attraction for the humanists of Lorenzo's circle, and made him to devote his last days to the cause of Christ and the Frate.

SANDRO BOTTICELLI

Sandro was the fourth son and youngest child of a prosperous tanner, Mariano di Vanni dei Filipepi. In these days there were large tanneries on the banks of the Mugnone, a stream on the outskirts of the city, which M. Müntz compares with the Bièvre in modern Paris. Probably Mariano was the owner of one of these tanneries, but he lived with his large family of children and grandchildren in a house of the Via Nuova, now the Via Porcellana, in the Borgo Ognissanti, close to the Church of Santa Lucia. He seems to have been in comfortable circumstances, and owned both houses and lands in other parts of the town. All his sons were brought up to some trade. The eldest, Giovanni, born in 1420, was, like his father, a leather merchant, who acquired the nickname of *Il Botticello*, either from the barrel which was the sign of his shop, or from his own corpulent figure.

The second, Antonio, was a goldsmith and bookseller, who afterwards settled at Bologna. The third, Simone, born in 1443, went to Naples at the age of fourteen, in the service of Paolo Rucellai, a wealthy Florentine banker. And the fourth, Sandro, seems to have been only about a year younger than Simone. In an income-tax return of February 1458 (O.S. 1457) which has lately been discovered by Mr. Herbert Horne, Sandro is described as being thirteen years of age, and as still going to school, on account of his delicate health. Vasari tells us that Sandro took no pleasure in reading, writing, or figures, and was always discontented, until his father, seeing the boy's eccentric habits, apprenticed him to a goldsmith named Botticelli, which was the origin of the nickname which clung to the painter throughout his life. But there seems to have been no goldsmith of that name in Florence ; and the surname of Botticelli, by which the artist became known to posterity, was evidently

11

acquired from his elder brother, the broker Giovanni. On the only two occasions in which he signed his works, he gives his name as Alessandro or Sandro di Mariano ; but alike in contracts and income-tax returns, he is generally described as *detto Botticello*, or *di Botticelli*. This evidently was the name commonly used by his comrades. Leonardo da Vinci speaks of him in his " Trattato " as " our Botticello " ; and Michelangelo, who was thirty years younger, sent a letter to him bearing the address of Sandro Botticelli. Antonio Billi, writing early in the sixteenth century, describes the painter as Sandro di Botticello ; while the Anonimo of the Codex Gaddiano, who compiled his record a few years later, gives his full name as " Sandro di Mariano di Vanni Filipepi, called Sandro di Botticelli."

It is, of course, possible that Sandro may have worked for a year or two with his brother, the goldsmith Antonio, but before long he succeeded in persuading his father that painting was his true vocation.

" The boy," writes Vasari, " was enamoured of painting, and opened his heart freely to his father, who, seeing the force of his inclination, took him to Fra Filippo of the Carmine, a most excellent painter of those days, in order that Sandro might learn from him according to his desire. From that time he devoted himself wholly to the study of this art, and followed and imitated the style of his master so closely, that Fra Filippo loved him dearly, and took so much pains in teaching him, that Sandro soon reached an excellence far beyond expectation."

Botticelli was probably apprenticed to Fra Filippo about 1460, when he was fifteen or sixteen, and accompanied the Carmelite to Prato, when four years later, by order of Cosimo dei Medici's illegitimate son

12

MADONNA DELLA VANNELLA (SETTIGNANO).

Carlo, the newly appointed Provost of the Collegiate Church, he resumed his long-neglected work in the Pieve. This ancient choir, where the genial friar painted his series of frescoes from the lives of St. Stephen and St. John the Baptist, was the true school in which the dreamy, impressionable lad received his artistic training.

In these fascinating, but sadly injured paintings, which still charm us by their brightness and animation, we recognize many of the motives which his scholar was to turn to good account in years to come. In the venerable evangelists, whose patriarchal figures look down from the vaulted roof; in the light and graceful steps of the dancing Salome, in her swaying form and fluttering draperies; in the yearning faces of the sorrowing disciples who stand round the bier of the first martyr; we already see the germ of Botticelli's art. And it is precisely in the last subjects of the series—the Feast of Herodias and the Stoning and Burial of St. Stephen—that we trace the strongest resemblance to the younger master's style. These frescoes were painted in 1464, when the reckless friar was working with feverish haste to make up for lost time and recover the favour of his indignant patrons.

Early in 1465 the long-delayed work was at length completed, and soon afterwards Botticelli returned to Florence. He did not accompany the Carmelite friar when, in March 1467, he set out on his last journey, to decorate the cupola of the Duomo at Spoleto. But the singing and dancing angels scattering roses at the feet of the blessed, which are so prominent a feature in Fra Filippo's fresco of Paradise, bear a striking likeness to some of Botticelli's creations and show that the pupil was familiar with the latest phase of his master's art. He may have helped the friar in preparing the cartoons for this important work, or, as is

13

more probable, may have visited Spoleto on his way to Rome in 1481. In any case Sandro did not forget the debt that he owed to his old master, and when after Filippo Lippi's death the Friar's young son was brought back to Florence, he entered Botticelli's studio and received his early training from his father's most distinguished pupil. One interesting work of Sandro's first period has been lately discovered by Mr. Berenson and Mr. Herbert Horne in the little oratory of the Madonna della Vannella near Settignano. The wayside shrine which contained this damaged fresco was originally raised in honour of Our Lady, whose kindly influence the Tuscan peasants invoked to shield the vineyards and orchards on the hill of Settignano from hail and tempest. The plump and rosy child standing on his mother's knee recalls Fra Filippo's babes; but the droop of the Virgin's head, and the gentle melancholy of her expression, are already characteristic of Botticelli. The group bears a marked resemblance to the Madonna and Child with the little St. John and the cypress and rose bushes in the background, now in the Louvre (No. 1296). This popular painting, which is still ascribed to Botticelli himself in the catalogue, was evidently executed by some follower, in the days when Sandro's fame was at its height, from one of his master's old drawings.

Another early work in which the best critics have long recognized Botticelli's hand and which he probably painted two or three years after the Settignano Madonna, is the long narrow panel of the Adoration of the Magi, now in the National Gallery (No. 592). Here the Virgin and Child are quite in Fra Filippo's style, but the crowd of spectators, the horses and pages on the left of the picture reveal the influence of a new teacher. This is none other than Antonio Pollaiuolo, the goldsmith-painter whose

Houghton.

JUDITH (UFFIZI).

marvellous powers of drawing exerted so powerful an influence on all the great masters of the next generation from Botticelli and Leonardo to Raphael and Michelangelo. After Fra Filippo's departure, Sandro was, it is plain, closely connected with both Antonio and his brother Piero, and probably worked during several years as their assistant. In this capacity, somewhere about the year 1470, he painted his noble figure of " Fortezza," as a companion to the six Virtues already executed by the Pollaiuoli brothers for the tribunal of the Mercatanzia. " As a youth," writes Antonio Billi, the oldest of Sandro's biographers, " he made in the Mercatanzia a most beautiful Fortezza." Both Vasari and the Anonimo give us the same information ; and Albertini in his Memoriale of 1510, remarks that the six Virtues in the Mercatanzia are by the hand of Piero Pollaiuolo, adding, " the seventh is by Sandro."

There can, we think, be no doubt that the figure in question was painted by Sandro, although in this instance he followed the pattern before him so closely that even Morelli would not accept the panel as his work. His Fortitude is a young woman partly clad in armour, seated in a recess, on a throne of coloured marbles, and bearing a mace in her hands. The figure is executed in the same pale colouring and sculptural style as the six companion Virtues by the Pollaiuoli, her embroidered draperies and the variegated marbles of her throne are the same. But the attitude and expression are altogether Sandro's own. The bent head and nervously clasped hands, the patient and weary but still resolute mien, all help to give the same impression of restrained force, of brave and steadfast endurance. We are reminded of the eloquent passage in which Ruskin long ago described this picture.

" Worn somewhat and not a little weary, instead of standing ready for all comers, she is sitting apparently in reverie, her fingers playing restlessly and idly—nay, I think even nervously—about the hilt of her sword. For her battle is not to begin to-day, nor did it begin yesterday. Many a morn and eve have passed since it began ; and now is this to be the ending day of it ? And if this—by what manner of end ? This is what Sandro's Fortitude is thinking, and the playing fingers about the sword hilt would fain let it fall, if it might be ; and yet how swiftly and gladly will they close on it, when the far-off trumpet blows, which she will hear through all her reverie."

The same fine, imaginative conception marks the other pictures which the young Florentine master painted at this period of his career. Foremost among these are the two small panels of Judith and Holofernes which Borghini, the eighteenth-century writer, mentions as having been given by Messer Ridolfo Sirigatti to the Grand Duchess Bianca Capello for her cabinet of paintings. Both of these little pictures are now in the Uffizi, and in spite of clumsy restoration are characteristic examples of Botticelli in his Pollaiuo-lesque time. In the one, Judith, bearing a sword in her right hand and an olive branch in her left, walks swiftly and lightly across the open hillside, attended by a faithful handmaid carrying her vessels of wine and oil in the one hand and the head of Holofernes, wrapt in a cloth on her head. Judith has the same long neck and peculiar type of face as the Fortezza, the same high cheek-bones and wistful eyes. Her countenance wears the same expression of gentle sadness, and the eyes of the servant are fixed in silent devotion on her mistress, as, strong in the might of the great deliverance that she has wrought, she returns to the tents of Israel. In the other panel, we see the tent of Holofernes, as it was on that same dread morning, with the curtains drawn back and the soldiers and servants looking in grief and horror at the headless corpse. The scene is painted with dramatic truth and vividness, and the drawing and modelling of the nude figures show how much Botticelli had learnt from the Pollaiuoli.

The same attempt to render the human form with truth and dignity is evident in the noble *St. Sebastian* which Sandro painted, according to Vasari, by order of Lorenzo dei Medici, for the Church of Santa Maria Maggiore, in January 1473–74. If this date, given by the Anonimo, is correct, Botticelli's *St. Sebastian* was finished before the famous version of the Saint's martyrdom, which Antonio Pollaiuolo executed in 1475, for the Pucci chapel in the Church of the Annunziata, and which is now in our National Gallery. The subject was a favourite one with the Florentine naturalists who readily embraced this opportunity of displaying their knowledge of anatomy and modelling. But Sandro was not content with this, and if his *St. Sebastian* fails to attain Antonio's mastery of structural design, the calm beauty of the martyr's face reveals the poetry and elevation of the young artist's thought. We have another proof of Sandro's romantic invention, in the fine landscape background, with its steep rocks and towers on the shore of a distant sea, which was to serve as a model for many of his contemporaries and followers in future days.

Closely akin to these works is the lovely Madonna which Morelli discovered twenty years ago in a dark corner of Prince Chigi's palace in Rome. Since then its sale has been the object of a notorious law-suit, and the picture is now the property of Mrs. J. L. Gardner of Boston, U.S.A. There is a youthful charm and *naïveté* about this little work, together with a certain delicacy and refinement, and a mystic vein of poetry, which renders it very attractive, while its excellent preservation lends it an especial value. A boy-angel robed in green, with a wreath of bay-leaves in his fair locks, is in the act of offering a bunch of grapes and wheat to the child on his mother's knee. The Virgin looks down pensively as she plucks one of the ripe ears of corn, and seems to muse thoughtfully over these symbols of the Eucharist, which the child in her arms blesses with his little hand. The composition of the group, the open window at the back with its charming glimpse of wooded hills and winding stream, the soft rose and pale-blue tints of the Madonna's draperies, and the transparent veil on her rippling hair all recall Fra Filippo's style, while in the fine modelling of the forms, especially that of the angel's face, Botticelli comes nearer to Pollaiuolo, in his attempt to attain structural completeness, than in any other work of this period.

There was another young Florentine painter with whom Sandro must have been intimately acquainted in these early years. This was Leonardo da Vinci, who was growing up in Andrea del Verrocchio's workshop and who was admitted into the Guild of Painters in the year 1472. Although eight years younger than Botticelli, Verrocchio's pupil already gave signs of genius that was to distinguish him among his fellows, and certain qualities in his art must early have excited Sandro's interest. We know that the two masters were friends at this period of their career, and though the character of their art differed in many respects, they were alike in their constant endeavour to attain ideal beauty and to give expression to the inner life of the soul. There can be little doubt that they influenced each other mutually, although the precise nature and degree of that influence is a problem that still remains to be solved. But the expression of the angel in the Chigi Madonna shows that Sandro was already striving to depict the finer and more subtle shades of feeling in his art, an effort which may have been prompted by his intercourse with Leonardo.

Meanwhile the originality of Sandro's own genius could not fail to command the attention of the cultured society of Florence in the days of the Medici.

When, in 1472, Fra Diamante, the Carmelite assistant who had followed Fra Filippo Lippi to Spoleto, returned to Florence after finishing his master's work, Botticelli was already known as an artist of reputation. His fame soon spread beyond the walls of his native city, and a few months after he had completed his panel of *St. Sebastian* he was invited to help in the decoration of the Campo Santo of Pisa, upon which another Florentine master, Benozzo Gozzoli, had been engaged during the last six years. In May 1474 he paid his first visit to Pisa, and received a florin for the expenses of his journey from the superintendent of the Duomo works. The result of this interview was that Botticelli agreed to paint an *Assumption* for the chapel of the Incoronata in the Duomo, on condition that, if the work met with approval, he would be employed to paint the same subject on the walls of the Campo Santo. In July Sandro returned to Pisa, and began to execute this honourable commission. During the next three months the archives of the Cathedral chapter contain frequent entries of supplies of corn given to Sandro, surnamed Botticello, as well as of payments of money for ultramarine which he had procured from Florence. But after September 1474, Sandro's name no longer appears in the register, and we can only conclude that the work was abandoned and left unfinished, because, as Vasari writes, it did not satisfy either the painter or his employers. In all probability he was impatient to return to Florence, where his reputation was already secured, and where a series of new and important works was awaiting him.

II

1475—1480

WHEN Sandro Botticelli first opened a workshop and entered on his career as an independent master, a new and brilliant era was dawning for his native city of Florence. On the death of Piero il Gottoso in 1469, his elder son, Lorenzo, a youth of twenty, succeeded without opposition to the post of chief magistrate, which his father and grandfather had held before him. Both he and his younger brother, the tall and handsome Giuliano, had been carefully trained by the foremost scholars in all the learning of the day, and from the moment that he took up the reins of government, Lorenzo showed himself a generous and enlightened protector of art and letters. Marsilio Ficino and the older Platonists who had enjoyed Cosimo's favour, held meetings of their Academy in the Palace of the Via Larga, and celebrated Plato's birthday in the gardens of the Medici villa at Careggi, while younger scholars and poets were attracted to Florence by a patron whose love of antiquity was as genuine as their own, and who wrote Latin verses worthy to rank with their best productions. Architects and sculptors, painters and goldsmiths found in the Magnifico a splendid and liberal master who had inherited the proud traditions of his ancestors, and grudged no expenditure on public buildings or works of art.

SANDRO BOTTICELLI

Both as the pupil of Fra Filippo Lippi, that spoiled child of the Medici, and the assistant of the Pollaiuoli brothers who had been constantly employed by Cosimo and his cultured son Piero, Sandro needed no introduction to Lorenzo's notice. In 1474 he had, as we have seen, received a commission to paint a *St. Sebastian* for this august patron. After his return from Pisa, at the close of the year, he was employed to paint a banner for the Tournament held in January 1475, on the Piazza di Santa Croce. On this memorable occasion Giuliano, the darling of the Florentine people, who was distinguished by his prowess in all knightly exercises, entered the lists wearing a cape sewn with pearls and rubies, and a suit of shining silver armour, and mounted on a splendid charger with richly-embroidered and jewelled trappings. There, before the eyes of his adored mistress, the beautiful Simonetta Vespucci, he vanquished all his rivals, and bore off the prize amidst the acclamations of the assembled multitudes.

The device adopted by Giuliano and represented on the banner borne before him, as was customary in these jousts, is described in an account of the Tournament which has been recently discovered in the Magliabecchiana Library by Signor Giovanni Poggi. Here, painted on a blue ground, with a rising sun above her head, was a large figure of Pallas wearing a fine gold vest and white robe, and standing on burning olive boughs. In her right hand the goddess bore a lance, in her left, a shield with the head of Medusa, while the God of Love lay bound with gold cords to an olive-tree behind her. The name of the artist is not given but the description agrees exactly with that given by Vasari of a life-sized Pallas painted by Botticelli in the Medici Palace, standing on a device of burning branches. There is an evident allusion to

22

Houghton.

GIOVANNI DEI MEDICI (UFFIZI).

PORTRAIT OF A MEDICI LADY (FRANKFORT).

this Pallas in the following entry from the Inventory of the treasures contained in the Medici Palace at the time of Lorenzo's death : " In the room of Piero—a cloth (*panno*) set in a gold frame, about 4 *braccia* high by 2 wide, bearing a figure of Pa—(Pallas) with a burning shield and an arrow, by the hand of Sandro da Botticelli."

Unfortunately this banner has perished together with most of the other paintings of Sandro in the Medici Palace. Among these Vasari describes Bacchus lifting a flask of wine to his lips with both hands— " a figure full of animation,"—as well as two portraits which must have been the earliest works which he painted for the Medici. One of these was the portrait of Lucrezia Tornabuoni, the wise and gifted mother to whom Lorenzo was so deeply attached and whose death in 1482 he lamented so truly. The other was the portrait of " *la bella Simonetta !* " the fair Genoese maiden who at fifteen became the bride of Marco Vespucci, a devoted follower of the Medici, and was the object of Giuliano's romantic devotion. Lorenzo speaks of his friend's wife with sincere affection, and her charms and goodness were the favourite theme of Poliziano and all the courtly poets of his circle. " Among many excellent gifts," writes Poliziano, " she had the sweetest and most attractive manners, so that all those who enjoyed the privilege of her friendship, thought themselves beloved by her, and it seemed almost impossible that so many men could love her without exciting any jealousy, and so many women praise her without feeling any sense of envy." Both the profile of Simonetta in the Pitti, and the striking portrait of Giuliano himself in the Morelli Gallery at Bergamo, were formerly supposed to have been painted by Botticelli, but are now recognized as the work of an assistant, probably the unknown artist to whom

23

SANDRO BOTTICELLI

Mr. Berenson has given the name of Amico di Sandro.

The only Medici portrait by Botticelli's own hand that still remains in existence is one of Cosimo's younger and favourite son Giovanni, whose early death was so bitterly lamented by his aged father. Sandro's little picture of this popular personage must have been copied from some earlier work, probably one of the wax effigies that were often modelled from a cast taken after death. Giovanni is represented in a black vest with a scarlet cap on his fair curly locks and a view of the winding Arno in the background. And in order that there should be no mistake as to his family, he holds a medal of his father Cosimo in both his hands. Another portrait which Sandro must have painted about the same time is that of the young Florentine in the red cap with the broad forehead and thick curly locks, now in the National Gallery. We know nothing of this youth, or of his connexion with the painter, but his bright and pleasant countenance and keen intellectual air are rendered with a force and reality which cannot fail to kindle our interest and awake our curiosity.

Giovanni dei Medici's portrait appears again in Sandro's famous altar-piece of the *Adoration of the Magi*, now in the Uffizi. The subject was a favourite one with Sandro, who has left us several versions of the familiar story painted at different periods of his career, with the most varied intentions and surroundings. Sometimes he places the scene in a rocky wilderness, sometimes in the heart of a pine-forest. In some instances he introduces Roman arches and monuments or wide landscapes with mountains and sea-shore. In the Uffizi altar-piece the legend of the Three Kings becomes an apotheosis of the house of Medici; in a later work it is used as an opportunity

THE ADORATION OF THE MAGI (UFFIZI).

for celebrating Savonarola's dream of the New Jerusalem on earth. Last of all, it is transformed into a
mystic vision of the Celestial Country, where bright-
hued seraphs dance and sing on the clouds of heaven,
and angels welcome martyred saints to their embraces.

Two versions of the subject belong to the early days
when the influence of the Pollaiuoli was still the pre-
dominating feature of his art. The long panel (No.
592) in the National Gallery was, as we have seen,
painted about 1468, the *tondo* in the same collection
probably belongs to a somewhat later period and was
not finished until after his return from Pisa, in 1474.
The long-tailed peacock perched on the marble
pedestal, the dog sitting upon its haunches, the
trumpeters and Roman arches in the background,
recall Benozzo Gozzoli's crowded compositions, and
may have been suggested by that master's frescoes in
the Campo Santo. But the animated groups of youths
and the foreshortened horses with their rich harness
and trappings are all in the style which Sandro had
acquired from his intercourse with the Pollaiuoli.
This round may indeed be the identical *tondo* of the
Epiphany which Vasari saw in the house of the Pucci,
that family which was so closely connected with the
Medici, and for whom Antonio Pollaiuolo painted his
great *St. Sebastian* in 1475. Like the long panel on
the same subject in the National Gallery, this picture
is still ascribed to Filippino Lippi in the official
catalogue, but is undoubtedly the work of this more
illustrious master and was acquired with the well-
known *Nativity* of 1500, from the Fuller-Maitland
Collection. Several of the heads in the left-hand
corner of this *tondo* bear a marked resemblance to
those in the Uffizi *Adoration*, which was evidently
painted a year or two later, probably about 1476.

The first thing that strikes us in this little altar-piece

is the boldness and originality of the conception. Certain traditional features of the composition are still retained. The pent-house roof and the ruined arches are still here. The peacock spreads his tail over the rough-hewn walls of the stable of Bethlehem and the Star from the East sheds its heavenly lustre on the Holy Family. But the Virgin and Child, instead of being placed in a corner of the picture and surrounded with a crowd of worshippers, occupy a prominent position in the centre, and are raised on a higher plane than the Magi; while Joseph looks on from behind, leaning his head on his hand in tranquil meditation. The number of spectators is greatly reduced and the attendants are ranged in groups on either side. Immediately in front of the central group, kneeling devoutly at the feet of the Child, with their golden caskets in their hands, are the Three Kings from the far East.

In these three figures we recognize three illustrious members of the house of Medici. Cosimo is the venerable old man, wearing a dark green mantle, edged with fur and embroidered with gold, who bends down to kiss the foot of the Child with an expression of tender love, writes Vasari, mingled with a sense of satisfaction at having reached the goal of his long journey. In the second King, kneeling in the foreground, and clad in a scarlet robe lined with ermine, we recognize the massive features and dark hair of Piero il Gottoso, which Mino da Fiesole's marble bust in the Bargello has rendered familiar. The third King, robed in white, kneeling on Piero's right, and turning to speak to his brother, is Cosimo's younger son Giovanni. The portraits of other members and friends of the family may be discovered among the life-like heads of the little knot of courtiers who stand together in the left-hand corner of the picture.

SANDRO BOTTICELLI

Several critics have recognized Giuliano dei Medici in the youth with the jet black locks and melancholy countenance who stands immediately behind the kneeling Magi, and Lorenzo himself in the youth wearing a crimson doublet and clasping the hilt of his sword with both hands. But in neither of these do we find that close resemblance to the medals and busts of the youthful brothers which is so marked in the case of their grandfather and his sons, and which justifies Vasari in declaring that this portrait of Cosimo is the most life-like and natural that was ever painted.

One other figure in the picture, however, is undoubtedly a portrait. This is the tall man with hooked nose and dark curling locks, who stands in the right-hand corner, wrapt in a long orange cloak. This is clearly the portrait of Sandro himself, whom we see here standing in a characteristic attitude, looking back over his shoulder, and fixing his keen gaze upon us. The powerful head, shaggy locks, and deep-set eyes, all give the impression of a man of strong character and great intellectual force, and bear a striking likeness to the portrait introduced by his pupil, Filippino, eight or nine years later, into a fresco of the Brancacci Chapel.

The scientific arrangement of the whole composition, the skilful manner in which the separate groups are balanced, the masterly modelling and life-like expression of each individual head in the picture, help to explain the enthusiastic admiration which Botticelli's *Adoration* excited among his contemporaries. " It is impossible," writes Vasari, " to describe the beauty which Sandro has imparted to each different figure and face. They are all placed in different positions. Some are seen full face, others in profile, others again at three-quarters, while some are looking

27

down. The variety of expression is infinite. Young and old alike are represented with an individuality that reveals the perfect mastery to which the artist had attained. . . . Alike in drawing, colour and composition, the work is so admirable and beautiful that every painter of our time is filled with wonder at the sight."

The date of this altar-piece and the introduction of the Medici portraits has, not unnaturally, led modern writers to conclude that this painting was presented by Lorenzo dei Medici to the church of Santa Maria Novella as a thank-offering for his escape from the assassins who murdered his brother Giuliano. But there is no evidence in support of this theory, and Mr. Horne has recently discovered documents which prove that this *Adoration* was originally painted for the family altar of Giovanni Lami, a merchant of a good old Florentine house, who availed himself of this opportunity to pay a graceful compliment to the powerful Medici. We learn from an eighteenth-century record that this altar, richly adorned with fine marble and carving, stood on the left of the great doors of Santa Maria Novella, and became known as the altar of the Epiphany, " from the picture of the *Three Kings*, painted by that most excellent master, Sandro Botticelli, and held by all to be a marvellously fine work."

Albertini, who wrote in Sandro's lifetime, Antonio Billi and the Anonimo Gaddiano all mention the altar-piece of the *Magi* by Sandro Botticelli as hanging on one side of the great doors in this church. It remained there until, in 1570, the ancient altar of the Lami family was removed and the picture sold to Fabio Mondragone, a Spanish chamberlain in the service of the Grand Duke Francis I. Five years later, Fabio fell into disgrace and his palace and effects were sold.

GROUP FROM THE "ADORATION OF THE MAGI" (UFFIZI).

Houghton.

PORTRAIT OF BOTTICELLI FROM THE "ADORATION OF
THE MAGI" (UFFIZI).

Then Sandro's *Adoration* passed into the Grand Duke's collection, and remained at the villa of Poggio Imperiale until it was removed to the Uffizi in 1796.

But if this altar-piece was not executed by the Magnifico's own orders, it no doubt attracted his attention and that of his powerful friends, and assured Sandro's place among the foremost masters in Florence. From that time he became the chosen painter of the Medici and was employed almost exclusively in their service during the next few years. He was now called upon to give another proof of his power in a new direction. That enthusiasm for the old Greek world which was the master-passion of the age, and which found so congenial a home among the poets and humanists of Lorenzo's immediate circle, had already fired the imagination of the best Florentine artists. Donatello reproduced the motives of classical story in the medallions with which he adorned the inner court of the palace of the Via Larga, and the Pollaiuoli brothers painted the *Labour of Hercules* on the walls. And Sandro's poetic and impressionable nature was quick to respond to those new influences, and to feel the charm of the old myths which had so powerful a fascination for the finest minds of his age. Antonio Billi and the Anonimo both tell us that he painted many figures of nude women that were surpassingly beautiful. The last-named writer further informs us that many of this master's finest works were to be seen in his day at Castello, the villa of Signor Giovanni dei Medici—that is to say, the famous captain known as "Giovanni *delle bande nere*," who was killed in a skirmish at Mantua in 1426. Vasari, who wrote thirty or forty years later, tells us that, in his time, these pictures were at Castello, a villa belonging to Giovanni's son, Duke Cosimo I. "One of them," he adds, "is a new-born Venus, who is blown to the shore by the winds and zephyrs. The other, a Venus wreathed with flowers by the Graces to represent Spring; and both of these he painted with rare grace."

In all probability these two pictures which the Anonimo and Vasari both saw in the villa of Castello were painted for Lorenzo di Pier Francesco, the head of the younger branch of the Medici, and grandson of Cosimo's only brother. This young man had lately succeeded to a large fortune on the death of his father, Pier Francesco, a partner in the Medici bank and a loyal supporter of Piero il Gottoso and his sons. The Magnifico was especially anxious to retain the friendship of this wealthy kinsman, who gave him financial help on more than one occasion and was on intimate terms with his cousins, both of whom were some years older than himself. Lorenzo di Pier Francesco shared their literary tastes, wrote songs and Latin verses, and was a generous patron of scholars and artists. This beautiful villa of Castello on the heights above Careggi, looking over the valley of the Arno, was the scene of many splendid fêtes and entertainments, in which the Magnifico himself and all the gilded youth of Florence took part. To him Poliziano dedicated the first of his Sylvæ, a poem entitled " Manto," in praise of Virgil, as well as an idyll on the charms of rural life at the Medici villa of Poggio a Cajano. Nothing was therefore more natural than that this wealthy and accomplished youth should wish to decorate his villa with pictures painted by Sandro's hand, on themes suggested by Poliziano.

The young humanist who stood so high in the Magnifico's favour and whom he afterwards chose for his son's tutor, had lately composed an epic in honour of Giuliano's Tournament. As Luigi Pulci, some years before, had celebrated Lorenzo's Giostra in

SPRING (ACCADEMIA, FLORENCE).

verse, so Poliziano now devoted his Muse to sing the arms and loves of the gallant Giuliano. After extolling the chivalrous deeds of his hero and the charms of the fair Simonetta, the poet takes us to the isle of Cyprus, and describes the Garden of Venus and the coming of Spring in melodious verse.

This was the passage which Botticelli chose to be the subject of his first painting, *La Primavera*, and which he no doubt executed with the help and advice of Poliziano. It was, we know, the habit of these Renaissance lords and ladies to employ scholars to arrange the details of the pictures which they ordered. Isabella d'Este invariably applied to some well-known humanist of her Court, Pietro Bembo or Paride da Ceresara, and desired them to supply Giovanni Bellini or Perugino with minute directions for the *fantasie* which were to adorn the walls of her studio. And Poliziano himself took a keen interest in artistic questions, and was intimately connected with some of the chief Florentine masters. He it was who published Alberti's "Treatise on Painting," and suggested the Battle of the Centaurs to young Michelangelo as a subject for one of his first bas-reliefs. He was also employed by Lorenzo to compose the epitaphs of Giotto and Fra Filippo Lippi, and wrote the inscription on Ghirlandajo's frescoes in Santa Maria Novella for the Tornabuoni. In this case, he probably discussed the details of the picture, which Sandro was to paint for the halls of Castello, with Lorenzo di Pier Francesco and his friends ; and the Magnifico himself, as the leader of fashion and arbiter of taste in Florence, no doubt took a prominent part in the discussion.

Poliziano's description of the enchanted realm where Venus reigns has been closely followed by the painter. Here, under a grove of orange-trees laden with golden fruit, encircled by a luxuriant growth of myrtle, the

Queen of Love holds her Court. Tall of stature, and majestic in bearing, robed in draperies of white and gold, and carrying a red mantle on her arm, she advances to welcome the coming of Spring, a beauteous maiden who steps lightly over the grass, bearing a lapful of roses, which she scatters before her as she goes. Her fair hair is wreathed with blue cornflowers and daisies ; her white robe is garlanded with long trails of fresh ivy and briar rose, and patterned over with flowers of every hue. Close on her footsteps follows the laughing nymph Flora, dropping rose-buds and anemones from her lips, as she flies from the ardent embrace of Zephyr, the blue-robed god who tries to seize her in his arms, exactly as described by Lorenzo, in a passage of the " Selve d'Amore," which he has evidently borrowed from the Latin poet Lucretius. On the left, the Three Graces clad in white draperies of transparent gauze, dance with hands linked together and arms entwined, on the dewy lawn. Mercury, a stalwart youth wearing a winged helmet over his thick black locks and a red drapery round his strong limbs, goes before and scatters the clouds of Winter with the rod in his hands, all unconscious of the golden shaft which the little Cupid who hovers in the air above, is aiming at his heart.

All the different elements which we find in Sandro's early works are present in this picture. The tall and slender figures and oval faces are of his peculiar type ; the light, clinging draperies and the rhythmical movement of the dancing maidens recall Fra Filippo's angels ; the rich embroideries and pearl-sewn tresses of Venus display that love of ornament which he had learnt in the goldsmith-painter's shop ; and the smile on the face of Spring has the subtle charm which haunts his friend Leonardo's creations. But what strikes us most of all in Sandro's painting is that new-

Houghton

THE THREE GRACES FROM "SPRING"
(ACCADEMIA, FLORENCE).

ONE OF THE GRACES FROM "SPRING"
(ACCADEMIA, FLORENCE)

born joy in the gladness of spring and the beauty of nature which speaks in every delicate bud and tender leaf, and which makes this picture so perfect an image of the delicious May-time which Lorenzo and his comrades were never tired of praising in their songs. The old classical myth is blended with the new modern spirit, and transfigured by the poet's fancy into a fairy dream of the young Renaissance.

Even to-day, when time and neglect have darkened the soft blue of the sky and the glossy verdure of orange and myrtle leaves, and dimmed the bright hues of fruits and flowers, Sandro's *Primavera* remains one of the most radiant visions that has ever dawned on the heart of a poet-painter. How much more must the loveliness of the young Florentine master's painting have called forth the admiration of the humanists who met that joyous May-time in the fair gardens of Castello ! But a tragic doom hung over these dreams of youth and love.

> *Quant' é bella giovinezza*
> *Che si fugge tuttavia !*
> *Chi vuol esser lieto sia,*
> *Di doman non c' è certezza.*

So, in the words of Lorenzo's Carnival hymn sang the gay revellers, all unmindful of the prophetic ring in the light refrain of their song, telling them how soon youth and joy must pass away. Before Poliziano had finished his poem, the fair Simonetta died of lingering consumption, and was borne to her grave in Ognissanti with her face uncovered, " that all," writes Lorenzo's friend Bettini, " might see her beauty, which was even greater in death than it had been in life." A great multitude of people followed her with tears, and all the poets of the Medici circle lamented her sad fate in song. Pulci and Poliziano composed Latin

c

elegies and epigrams, and Lorenzo himself wrote sonnets to her memory.

Two years later, on Sunday the 26th of April, 1478, her constant adorer, Giuliano, was murdered by the Pazzi conspirators during the celebration of mass in the Duomo, and fell pierced with nineteen wounds on the steps of the Choir. Lorenzo narrowly escaped the same fate, and was only saved by his own presence of mind and the courage of his servants, who dragged him into the sacristy and closed Luca della Robbia's bronze doors in the face of his pursuers. The Florentines rallied loyally round Lorenzo, and avenged Giuliano's murder with terrible promptitude. The conspirators were put to death, even the Archbishop of Pisa was hung from the windows of the Palazzo Pubblico, and Botticelli was employed to paint the effigies of the traitors on the walls outside.

In 1480, when peace had been restored and the dominion of the Medici was once more firmly established, Lorenzo desired Botticelli to commemorate the triumph of his house in a new painting. This was the famous group of *Pallas subduing the Centaur*, which was discovered eight years ago in a dark corner of the Pitti Palace. The only mention of the picture in contemporary records is to be found in an inventory of the Medici collections in the palace of the Via Larga taken in October 1516, where it is described as " a painting containing a figure of Minerva and a Centaur." But in this tall and stately Pallas armed with halberd and buckler seizing the Centaur by the forelock, it is clear that we have an allegory of the victory of the Medici and the restoration of their wise and beneficent rule. The white robe of the goddess is embroidered with the triple diamond ring that was the favourite device of the Medici. The graceful olive boughs wreathed about her brows and trailing

Houghton.

LA .BELLA SIMONETTA (PITTI).

Marcozzi.

GIULIANO DEI MEDICI (BERGAMO).

over her breast and arms are symbolic of the peace
which Lorenzo had succeeded in securing ; while the
Centaur, who had been the emblem of crime and
folly from the days of Giotto and Dante, in this case
fitly represents the Pazzi, whose name literally signifies
" fools." But Sandro's Centaur is no monster of vice
and ugliness. On the contrary, his venerable figure
and aged face seems to plead for mercy as he cowers
before this triumphant daughter of the gods standing
before us in the might of her divine youth and beauty.
The distant prospect of the Bay of Naples, with the
ship sailing across its waters, was evidently intended
to commemorate that successful mission to the Court
of King Ferrante, from which Lorenzo had just
returned, in February 1480, amidst the joyful acclamations of the Florentine people.

The general style of Botticelli's picture confirms the
supposition that it was painted about this time.
While the figure of Pallas resembles both the *Fortezza*
and the Venus of the *Primavera*, and still retains the
exaggerated curve of hip which is a curious feature of
Sandro's women at this period, the signs of the
Pollaiuoli's influence are less marked than in these
earlier works. Nowhere is his scheme of colour more
pleasing and harmonious than in this Pallas with the
rich green mantle falling over her white robe, the
orange sandals on her feet, and the bright red-gold
locks streaming on the breeze, against the background
of grey shelving rocks. So the painter once more
proved that poetic imagination can gild the dullest
theme with light, and transform even a political
cartoon into a thing of beauty.

Two other mythical subjects by Sandro's hand are
still in existence, although it is very doubtful if he
painted them before his journey to Rome, in the
early months of 1481. One of these is the *Birth of*

35

Venus which Vasari saw in the villa of Castello together with the *Primavera*. As in the case of the last-named picture, the composition was evidently derived from Poliziano's poem of the Giostra. In a passage adapted from one of the Homeric hymns, the poet tells us how the new-born Aphrodite was blown by the soft breath of the Zephyrs, on the foam of the Egean waves to shore. Heaven and earth, he sings, rejoice at her coming. The Hours wait to welcome her and spread a star-sown robe over her white limbs, countless flowers spring up in the grass where her feet will tread. All this exquisite imagery is faithfully reproduced in Sandro's painting. He has represented his Venus Anadyomene laying one hand on her snowy breast, the other on her loose tresses of golden hair—a form of virginal beauty and purity, as with feet resting on the golden shell she glides softly over the rippling surface of the waves. He has painted the winged Zephyrs hovering in the air linked fast together, blowing the goddess to the flower-strewn shore and the shower of single roses fluttering about her form. Only, instead of the three Hours of Homer's hymn and Poliziano's poem, he shows us one fair nymph, in a white robe, embroidered with blue corn-flowers, springing lightly forward to offer Venus a pink mantle sown with daisies. In the laurel groves along the shore, we see a courtly allusion to the " Laurel who sheltered the song-birds that carolled to the Tuscan spring," while in the background the eye roams across long reaches of silent sea to distant headlands sleeping under the cool grey light of early dawn.

The sense of light and airy movement is wonderfully given in wind-blown draperies and falling roses, in rippling waves and tossing locks, in the swift action and glad gesture of the welcoming nymph, in the gliding motion of Venus herself. Sandro himself has

36

PALLAS (PITTI).

never fashioned a fairer or more delicate form than this goddess whose ivory limbs may well have been modelled, as tradition says, from some antique marble in the Medici garden. In this masterpiece we feel that the painter has freed himself wholly from the influence of others and relies entirely on his own resources. The stiffness and rigidity of his early works have given way to perfect ease and grace, to a beauty of line and decorative completeness which has been rarely surpassed by the most consummate artist.

The other classical subject which Sandro painted about the same time, is the panel of *Mars and Venus* in the National Gallery. This time one of the Magnifico's own poems was the theme of his picture, which probably adorned a doorway in the Medici Palace, and remained in Florence until it came to England in the Barker Collection some fifty years ago. " The Loves of Mars and Venus " was the title of one of the curious dramatic compositions which Lorenzo wrote and may have been performed by his own children on some festive occasion. It consists of four monologues spoken in turn by Venus, Mars, Apollo and Vulcan, and contains some of Lorenzo's best and sweetest verse. In his painting Sandro represents the broad-chested, strong-limbed god of war reclining on the flowery sward, as with his head drowsily sunk back, he slumbers in the cool shade of the myrtle bowers on the shores of the summer sea, that *dolce ospizio* which is described in the poet's verse. Four little goat-footed loves play with his lance and helmet, and one mischievous boy blows through a shell in the sleeping warrior's ear without apparently producing the least effect. These sportive children were evidently suggested by a passage in Lucian's description of a picture of the *Marriage of Alexander* by Aëtion. The Greek poet whose minute and critical account of works

37

of art was very popular with Florentine humanists, exactly describes the three little Cupids carrying the hero's spear while he slumbers, which we see in Sandro's picture. On the opposite side Venus herself, clad in a white gold-braided robe, and resting her arm on a crimson pillow, sits up erect and grave, watching her lover with an air of contented repose. The careful arrangement of the goddess's curled and plaited locks, her life-like and expressive features, have led one distinguished critic, Dr. Richter, to suppose that we have here a portrait of Simonetta, and that the sleeping god is none other than her lover the *bel Giuliano*. This conjecture may not commend itself to all, but there can be no question as to the rare decorative charm of the design, the admirable modelling of the war-god's limbs, the incomparable beauty of line revealed in living forms and flowing draperies, or the rich colouring of crimson cushions, gold-chased armour and green myrtles seen against the soft tints of sky and sea.

The companion panel to this picture (No. 916), a Venus reclining on a couch, while three *Amorini* play at her feet with bunches of grapes and red and white roses, which was also acquired by the National Gallery at the Barker sale, is now recognized as the work of Jacopo del Sellajo, one of Sandro's most skilful assistants, who has recently been the subject of critical studies from the pens of Mrs. Berenson and Herr Hans Mackowsky.

THE BIRTH OF VENUS (UFFIZI)

III

1480—1482

IN 1480, the year in which Botticelli painted his *Pallas and the Centaur* to commemorate Lorenzo's safe return from Naples, he was employed by the dead Simonetta's relatives, the Vespucci, to paint a fresco of *St. Augustine* in the nave of Ognissanti, their parish church. " There," writes Vasari, " Sandro put forth his greatest powers to surpass all his contemporaries, but especially Domenico Ghirlandajo, who had painted a *St. Jerome* on the opposite wall." This work proved worthy of the highest praise and he succeeded in showing, in the head of this Saint, that profound depth and acuteness of intellect which marks those wise and thoughtful men who are continually engaged in the study of high and difficult subjects. Ghirlandajo, as Vasari intimates, was at this time Sandro's chief rival in the favour of the Medici and the leading families of Florence. But the style and temperament of the two masters was curiously unlike, and the contrast is nowhere more evident than in the frescoes which may still be seen side by side in Ognissanti.

Both Saints are represented sitting at their writing-desks, engaged in profound meditation. But while Ghirlandajo is wholly intent on the external aspect of his theme, and renders every detail—the candle and hour-glass, the inkstand and scissors, the Cardinal's hat and flask on the shelf, even the variegated pattern of the table-cloth—with Dutch-like accuracy, Botticelli after his wont takes us into the heart of his subject and lays bare the working of the great scholar's mind. He realizes with penetrating sympathy the fiery zeal and ardent devotion of the Saint of Hippo, whom he shows us sitting in his lonely cell, with worn face and deeply-furrowed brows, pondering over the problems which perplex his soul, while his upturned eyes and parted lips seem to breathe a prayer to heaven for light.

In this same year, 1480, which was so full of great enterprises, a second income-tax return gives us a glimpse into Sandro's private life. The painter we find is still living in the home of his old father in the Via Nuova. Mariano himself is described as eighty-six years of age, and too old to work—*non fa più nulla*. But his large family of children and grand-children are for the most part still living under the paternal roof, and in order to make room for these twenty souls he rents another house next to his own at nine florins a year. His wife is dead and her sister, Monna Vangelista, aged seventy, the widow of Mariano's brother Amedeo, now manages the household. The eldest son, Giovanni, surnamed Botticello, aged sixty, carries on business as a merchant of leather, and has a family of seven children, by his wife Monna Nera, the daughter of Benincasa dei Chori. Of these the eldest, Benincasa, a youth of nineteen, is in Rome with the banker Salviati, but costs his parents more money than he earns. Amedeo, aged eleven, is employed in a bank and has good prospects, but does not yet earn a single *maravedi*! Agnoletto, aged eight, and Jacopo, aged three, go to school, and the three girls Alessandra, Anna and Smeralda, an infant in arms, are as yet unprovided with dowries. The second brother,

40

SANDRO BOTTICELLI

Antonio, aged fifty-one, formerly a goldsmith, is now living at Bologna, where he sells books and makes about two florins a month, besides expenses, and has three children, a girl Elisabetta, aged nine, and two boys, Mariano, aged seven, who afterwards became an artist and died in 1527, and Bartolommeo, aged five. His wife, Bartolommea Spigolati, is seven months with child. The third brother, Simone, is about forty-one years of age, is living in Naples without occupation. Finally there is Mariano's youngest son, the painter Sandro, who " works in the house when he chooses." His age is given as thirty-three, which does not agree with the statement that he was thirteen in the *catasto* of 1457, but these small discrepancies are common in Florentine registers, and as a rule the returns made in earlier years when a boy was still living at home under his mother's eye are the most trustworthy. In spite of the usual attempt to plead poverty in the eyes of the law, it is plain that the family were in comfortable circumstances. Mariano had inherited property from his brother Jacopo, also a tanner, who had died child-less, and owned houses and land at Peretola which produced seventy-two bushels of wheat and thirteen measures of wine in the year, and rented a farm at Careggi, for thirty florins, " where he might seek shelter in time of plague." This last fact deserves attention. It is of especial interest to know that Sandro's father had a country house at Careggi, close to Lorenzo's favourite villa, in these days when the painter was constantly working for the Magnifico and his friends and enjoyed the society of the distinguished scholars and poets who belonged to the Medici circle.

Early in the following year Sandro received an important commission from a new and unexpected quarter. He was invited by Pope Sixtus IV to super-intend the decoration of his newly-erected chapel in the Vatican. During many years this ambitious pontiff had been the bitterest enemy of the Medici. His nephew, Girolamo Riario, had been the prime mover in the plot which had cost Giuliano his life, and it was no secret that the Pazzi conspiracy had been hatched in the Vatican. When the Florentines in their just indignation hanged the Archbishop of Pisa and imprisoned Cardinal Raffaelle Riario, Sixtus IV retaliated by laying their city under an interdict which was only removed in December 1480. One of the first demands insisted on by the Pope at that time was the removal of the effigies of the Pazzi conspirators from the façade of the Palazzo. Now, by a singular fate, the very artist who had painted these effigies was invited to paint the papal chapel in the Vatican.

It has generally been supposed that Botticelli and his comrades were invited to Rome by the Pope's nephew, Cardinal Giuliano della Rovere, afterwards Pope Julius II, who visited Florence in June 1481, on his way to France. But by this time the Tuscan painters were already at work in the Sistina, and it is more probable that their names were suggested to the Pope by Giovanni Tornabuoni or Guido Antonio Vespucci, who were sent to Rome as envoys from the Republic in December 1480. Vasari, indeed, ascribes the Pope's invitation to the renown which Botticelli acquired by his altar-piece in Santa Maria Novella. "So great," he writes, "was the fame which this *Adoration* brought him both in Florence and beyond its walls, that Pope Sixtus, having built a chapel in his palace in Rome, and wishing it to be decorated with frescoes, appointed him to be overseer of the work."

But the Anonimo Gaddiano speaks of another *Adoration* which was painted during Botticelli's visit to Rome, and which "was held to be the finest of all his works." This, we have little doubt, was the

ADORATION OF THE MAGI (ST. PETERSBURG).

beautiful version of the subject which is now in the Hermitage at St. Petersburg. Both in colour and composition this little picture is a gem of the purest water. Fewer figures are introduced than in the Uffizi altar-piece, but these are instinct with life and passion, while there is none of the violent exaggeration which mars the painter's later works. The scene is laid in a lovely wide landscape, with distant mountains and sea, and the round arches and classical pillars which support the pent-house roof, as well as the prancing horses, which recall the famous group on Monte Cavallo, are evident signs of Sandro's presence in the Eternal City. Finally, in the vigorous young oak-trees growing on the right of the stable of Bethlehem, we recognize the device of the Della Rovere family, which Raphael was one day to introduce in the frescoes on the ceiling of the Camera della Segnatura. This picture may have been painted for Cardinal Giuliano, whose love of art was already well known, and may have been the *Adoration* which first attracted the Pope's notice and led him to choose Sandro to superintend the decoration of his own chapel.

All we know for certain is, that on the 27th of October, 1481, a contract was drawn up between the Florentine architect and pontifical Commissioner Giovannino dei Dolci and the four painters, Alessandro di Mariano, Cosimo Rosselli, Domenico Tommaso (Ghirlandajo) of Florence, and Pietro Perugino, of Città della Pieve, by which these masters agreed to paint ten frescoes in the Pope's new chapel by the following 15th of March. In this document mention is made of the subjects which had been already painted in this place by these masters, and of payments which they had received. And the papal secretary Jacopo di Volterra, a careful and trustworthy writer,

43

notes in his diary of 1481 that on the first Sunday in Lent, being the eleventh day of March, divine service was held in the Pope's apartments, since the chapel was being adorned with excellent and splendid works. We learn from the same annalist that at Christmas 1481 the chapel was not yet available for use, since, " as I have often said before, it is being decorated with sacred emblems and paintings."

The new chapel formed part of a block of buildings which the Florentine architect Giovannino dei Dolci added to the Vatican by the Pope's order, soon after his accession. It was a plain oblong building lighted by twelve round-headed windows in the upper part of the walls, which left the surface of the lower walls free for pictorial decoration. The builders' work was completed by the end of 1480, and the painters set to work early in the following year. Botticelli's actual share in the decoration of the chapel consisted in three historical frescoes, as well as some of the figures of the early Popes, which occupy the niches between the windows. In spite of their damaged condition, Sandro's hand can be clearly recognized in several of these portraits, and Dr. Steinmann ascribes no less than seven to him. That of Sixtus II, with his hand on his heart and his eyes raised to heaven, bears a marked resemblance to the *St. Augustine* which Botticelli had lately painted in Ognissanti, while both the figures of the venerable Stephanus Romanus and of the young and ascetic Cornelius appear to be his work.

The subjects of the historical frescoes were probably chosen by Sixtus IV himself, who had acquired considerable reputation as a theologian before his elevation to the Papacy. On the left wall we have six scenes from the life of Moses, who, as the leader of the chosen people, was a recognized type of Christ. On the right, six subjects from the life of Christ are seen.

44

SANDRO BOTTICELLI

Thus the outline of the chief events in the Jewish and Christian dispensation and the history of the founders of the old and new covenant are set forth on the walls of the Papal chapel. And, since the chapel was dedicated to Santa Maria dell' Assunta, the *Assumption of the Virgin* was to occupy a central place over the altar, between the *Birth of Christ* and the *Finding of Moses.* These three frescoes were assigned to Perugino, but were afterwards effaced under the pontificate of Paul III, to make room for Michelangelo's *Last Judgment.*

The first fresco on which Sandro was employed occupies the space on the right wall exactly opposite the Papal throne. The subject was nominally the *Temptation of Christ,* but the true intention, as Dr. Ernest Steinmann has recently explained, was the glorification of Pope Sixtus IV. The chief object in the centre of the picture is a noble Renaissance temple which agrees exactly with an old print of the hospital of San Spirito, an ancient foundation which the Pope had recently restored on a splendid scale. In front of this building the different ceremonies for the purification of a leper, as appointed by the law of Moses in the book of Leviticus, are successively illustrated. Immediately before the temple stands the altar with the burning cedar-wood, surrounded by a crowd of figures. The leper himself is led up the steps, supported by his friends. His wife advances hastily on the opposite side, carrying the offering of two doves in a basket on her head. In the foreground, the high priest receives a golden bowl from the hands of a young assistant, and dips the bunch of myrtle into the blood of the victim, with which the leper is to be sprinkled seven times. The mystical meaning attached to leprosy throughout the Old Testament as a type of sin, and the fact that the nursing of lepers was a duty

45

enjoined on his followers by St. Francis, the founder
of the Order to which the Pope belonged, render this
subject especially appropriate. In the group of spectators on the right, portraits of several prominent
personages of the Papal Court are introduced, probably
members of the Confraternity of S. Spirito, to which
the Pope and most of the Cardinals belonged. Among
these we recognize the hated Girolamo Riario, the
husband of Caterina Sforza, bearing his baton as
Gonfaloniere of the Church, and the dark eyes and
striking features of Cardinal Giuliano della Rovere.
In the beautiful young woman who swiftly moves
forward between these two figures with a bundle of
wood on her head, we see a type which recurs frequently in Sandro's Florentine pictures ; and the boy
at her side carrying a bunch of grapes and looking
down in alarm at the snake which is coiled round his
leg, is an evident reminiscence of the *Girl with a
Serpent* in the Capitol Museum. In the background,
on the rocky heights overshadowed by the tall and
stately oak-trees of the Della Rovere family, the
different episodes of the Temptation of Christ are
introduced, in conformity with the general scheme of
decoration. On the left, Satan, clad in Franciscan
garb, with the cloven hoof and bat's wings peeping
out from under his habit, points to the stones at the
feet of Christ, and asks Him to command that they
should be made bread. In the centre of the picture
he appears again, standing on the topmost pinnacle of
the Renaissance temple, and desires the Son of God
to cast Himself down. Finally, on the right-hand
corner of the fresco, Christ is seen on the top of the
high mountain, lifting His hand with commanding
gesture, and bidding the tempter begone. At His
word, Satan, casting aside his friar's habit, staff and
rosary, plunges headlong into the abyss, and angels

46

place bread and wine on a table covered with a fair white linen cloth, and minister to their Lord.

Botticelli's second fresco on the *Life of Moses* includes no less than seven episodes from the early history of the Law-giver, which had to be combined in a single work. Out of this unpromising material the painter has contrived to make a singularly beautiful picture. With true artistic feeling he seizes on the most picturesque incident in the story—the meeting of Moses with the daughters of Jethro at the well— and groups the other episodes round this central subject. We see Moses, the dark-haired stranger, drawing water for the thirsty sheep from the well under the shady oak-trees, and the Midianite shepherds retreating hastily, while the fair shepherdesses look with shy gratitude in their eyes at the chivalrous Hebrew who has come to their help. Zipporah, the daughter of Jethro, with her tall, graceful form, gentle face, and fair hair wreathed with myrtle, bearing the distaff and apple branch in her hand, is one of Sandro's most attractive creations, and the whole scene is a simple and charming idyll of pastoral life. The other episodes are skilfully arranged on the hillside in the background, so as not to interfere with the central motive. On the right we see Moses in the act of slaying the Egyptian, and flying into the wilderness to escape from the wrath of Pharaoh. Further on, he is taking the shoes from off his feet and kneeling before the burning bush to hear the word of the Lord. Finally, in the foreground, on the left of the picture, he is seen leading the chosen people out of Egypt, followed by his wife and family. Among these, Aaron is a conspicuous figure, with his black beard and Oriental turban ; one fair-haired boy carries a white dog, and a little child looks up at his mother with the appealing gaze that Sandro has often repeated in his pictures of the infant Christ. Unfortunately this fresco has been sadly injured by the erection of the baldacchino over the Papal throne, and the figures on the right-hand portion are repainted.

The Punishment of Korah, Dathan and Abiram is the subject of Sandro's third and last fresco. " Let no man take office upon himself, unless he be called of God, as Aaron was." These words of the Latin text, inscribed on the Arch of Constantine, which is introduced in the centre of the picture, strike the key-note of the subject which is supposed to have been suggested by the revolt of the Archbishop of Krain, the Hungarian prelate who dared to proclaim a general council at Bâle in March 1482, and openly denounce Pope Sixtus as a " child of the devil." A retribution as swift and sudden as the judgment of Korah soon overtook him and his friends, and Botticelli's fresco was painted opposite Perugino's *Delivery of the Keys to St. Peter*, to commemorate this fresh proof of the divine authority which was committed to the successors of the Prince of the Apostles. The grand and imposing figure of Moses, who, standing before the altar, lifts his rod and calls down the wrath of God on the conspirators, lends a certain unity to the composition which is lacking in Sandro's other Sistine frescoes, and the destruction of the guilty intruders is rendered with dramatic vigour. One is struck down in the act of approaching the altar of sacrifice, another falls back with a cry of terror, and a third lies prostrate on the ground, while Aaron is seen standing behind the altar in his triple tiara calmly swinging his own censer, and his son Eleazar scatters the sacrilegious fire from the vessels on the altar. On the right, one of the blasphemers is dragged away to die by a crowd of indignant men armed with stones ; on the left, Moses stands with uplifted arm above the open abyss which is in the act of swallowing Dathan and Abiram, while Eldad and Medad, robed in white, hover in the air, and prophesy in the name of the Lord. This fresco is remarkable for the richness of the costumes, the beauty of the landscape setting, and the noble colonnades which are introduced in the background. Both the figure and action of the youthful Eleazar are full of life and fire, and many heads of striking individuality are introduced among the spectators. One of these— the second in the group on the right—is supposed by Dr. Steinmann to be the painter's own portrait. The finely-cut features and deep-set eyes have the same keen, eager expression as in the portrait of the Uffizi *Adoration*, and his black cap and dark vest are conspicuous by their simplicity among the scarlet robes and splendid apparel of cardinals and Church dignitaries.

These three frescoes, which Botticelli painted on the walls of the Sistina during the years 1481 and 1482, are among his most remarkable achievements. They reveal at once the influence which the classical monuments of ancient Rome produced upon his art, his increased mastery in the rendering of form and movement and his power as a creative and original genius. And they show his supremacy among his contemporaries, whether Florentine or Umbrian. It is true that the works which he painted in the Pope's chapel fall short in some respects of those executed by his fellow-artists. They lack the calm repose and wide spaces of Perugino's compositions and the symmetrical arrangement and unity which lend a certain grandeur to Ghirlandajo's more prosaic creations. But in wealth and variety of imagination, in beauty of form and picturesque detail, in vigorous action and intensity of emotion, Sandro's compositions far excel those of his rivals.

D

SANDRO BOTTICELLI

The Pope, no mean authority in works of art, was well satisfied and, Vasari tells us, rewarded Sandro liberally, recognizing that he had surpassed all his peers and acquired greater fame and renown than any of the competitors. "Unfortunately," continues the biographer, "Sandro, with his usual recklessness, spent all that he had earned in Rome and then returned suddenly to Florence." That Botticelli set little store on money we can well believe, but Vasari's account of his extravagant and idle habits is probably as exaggerated as his repeated assertions that the painter abandoned his work and consequently fell into dire poverty in his later years. The historian does justice, however, to Sandro's genial temper and to the great affection which he cherished, not only for his own pupils, but for all those who were ardent students of art. He was popular with all the young painters in Florence. Even scholars in the rival workshop, young Michelangelo and Bartolommeo di Giovanni, who both received their early training from Ghirlandajo, were on friendly terms with Sandro, and the latter worked for many years as his assistant. And the most distinguished of all his pupils, Filippino, showed his affection by introducing a portrait of his master, standing a little apart from the other spectators, wrapt in a long mantle, in one of his first great works, the fresco of the *Crucifixion of St. Peter* in the Brancacci Chapel.

Vasari records for our benefit some of the merry sayings and practical jokes in which Sandro frequently indulged with his friends and pupils. On one occasion Biagio Tucci painted a replica of one of his master's works—a *tondo* of the Madonna and Child with eight angels—and Botticelli found him a customer who promised to return the next day and buy the picture for six gold florins. But in the night Sandro and another of his pupils, named Jacopo, with the help of a little wax, stuck eight red paper caps, such as those worn by the chief magistrates, on the heads of the angels, and when Biagio appeared the next morning with the purchaser, to his great surprise he saw his Madonna seated in the midst of the Signoria of Florence! The customer, however, made no objection, but purchased the picture, and taking Biagio back to his house, paid him the six florins. When Biagio returned to the *bottega*, he found that Sandro and Jacopo had removed the red caps in his absence, and in his amazement exclaimed, " My dear master, I know not if I am dreaming, but when I was here before these angels had red caps on their heads and now they have none. What can have happened ? " " Thou art beside thyself, it is clear, my poor Biagio ! " returned Sandro gravely, " this money has turned thy head ! " And the other scholars all said the same, so much so that Biagio himself began to think that he had been the victim of some hallucination of his own brain.

Another time, Botticelli, out of pure mischief, went to the vicar of his parish and accused one of his neighbours of holding the heretical opinions of the Epicureans and believing that the soul dies with the body. The accused was summoned before the ecclesiastical court to defend himself, and when he was confronted with Sandro, exclaimed, " It is true that I believe this man's soul will perish, and do you not take him to be a heretic also, since without learning and being hardly able to read, he has ventured to write a commentary on Dante ? " The anecdote is noteworthy as showing Botticelli's interest in theological questions and his well-known love of Dante, whose " Divina Commedia " he certainly studied with an attention which, according to Vasari, led him to neglect his own painting.

51

But the best of these stories is told by the Anonimo Gaddiano. One day his great friend, Messer Tommaso Soderini, Lorenzo dei Medici's cousin, was trying in vain to persuade Sandro to marry. "I will tell you," replied the painter, "what happened to me the other night. I dreamt that I was married, and the bare idea made me so miserable, that for fear I should fall asleep and dream the same dream over again, I got up and rushed about the streets of Florence all night, as if I were a madman! After that sally, Messer Tommaso saw that this was not the kind of soil to plant a vineyard in." A confirmed bachelor and pleasant companion, the best of masters and truest of friends, with a kind heart and keen sense of humour, full of sympathy for promising scholars and of love for little children, spending freely and giving largely, strong in his likes and dislikes, deeply religious but hating cant and hypocrisy, passionate in his enthusiasm for great leaders and lost causes—such was Sandro Botticelli, the favourite painter of Lorenzo dei Medici and the faithful follower of Savonarola.

IV

1482—1495

THE frescoes of the Sistine Chapel were not finally completed until the month of August 1483, but Botticelli probably finished his share in the work earlier and returned to Florence by October 1482, since, on the 5th of that month, he received a commission from the Signoria to adorn a hall in the Palazzo Pubblico with frescoes. Ghirlandajo, Perugino, and his own scholar, Biagio Tucci, were to be associated with him in the work, but we never learn if this commission was executed, and only know that in 1487, Sandro painted a *tondo* for the Hall of Audience of the Council of the Massari.

During the next few years he was chiefly engaged in working for the Magnifico, who employed him and his old rivals, Perugino and Ghirlandajo, as well as his own pupil, Filippino, to decorate the villa of Lo Spedaletto with another great series of frescoes. This villa, on the heights near Volterra, had formerly belonged to the Nursing Order of the Frati Ospitalieri of Siena, and was a favourite residence of Lorenzo, who, during the latter years of his life, regularly spent some weeks there during the autumn for the benefit of his health. At his death in 1492, he left the estate of the Spedaletto to his favourite daughter, Maddalena, the wife of Pope Innocent VIII's nephew, Francesco Cybò, of whom he speaks with so much affection in

his letters, and calls " the apple of her mother's eye."
From her descendants it passed one hundred years
later to the Corsini family, who are still the owners of
this old Medici villa. The importance of the works
that were executed here by Lorenzo's orders about
the year 1483 or 1484, is proved by a report that was
sent a few years later by a Milanese agent to Lodovico
Sforza. This prince, who had already taken Leonardo
into his service on the Magnifico's recommendation,
now asked his envoy to send him a list of the best
painters in Florence. After giving the names and
describing the respective merits of Botticelli, Filippino,
Perugino, and Ghirlandajo, the writer informs his
lord that " all the said masters, excepting Filippino,
have given proof of their excellence in the Chapel of
Pope Sixtus, and that all of them afterwards worked
in the Spedaletto of the Magnifico Lorenzo."

We learn from Vasari that one of the subjects
painted by Ghirlandajo in this villa was the *Forge of
Vulcan*, " with many nude figures welding the thunder-
bolts of Jove with mighty hammers." From this we
may conclude that the themes of the frescoes were
classical and that Lorenzo's dramatic poem of the
" Loves of Mars and Venus " was among the subjects
with which Sandro and his comrades decorated the
villa walls. But although a portion of the Spedaletto
is still standing, and a loggia in the courtyard retains
some traces of colour, the great hall was destroyed by
fire early in the last century, and nothing is now to be
seen by the hand of the gifted band of masters who
once worked within its walls.

A better fate has attended two of the frescoes which
Sandro painted at Chiasso Macerelli near Careggi, to
commemorate the wedding of young Lorenzo Tornabuoni with the beautiful Giovanna degli Albizzi. The
bridegroom was the son of the wealthy Giovanni

LORENZO TORNABUONI WELCOMED BY THE LIBERAL ARTS (LOUVRE)

SANDRO BOTTICELLI

Tornabuoni, the uncle of the Magnifico and his chief agent in Rome, and was himself a great favourite with Lorenzo and the leading humanists in Florence. To him, in the year 1486, Poliziano dedicated his poem of "Ambra" in a dedication extolling the young man's wide learning and excellent knowledge of Greek and Latin. When this accomplished youth led home the lovely bride whose delicate features and auburn ringlets live in Ghirlandajo's paintings, there was great rejoicing among the Medici and their friends. The two illustrious families vied with each other in the splendour of the banquets, torchlight dances and tournaments at which the guests were entertained. The Spanish ambassador to the Vatican was present at the wedding, which took place in the month of June 1486. While Giovanni Tornabuoni's favourite painter, Ghirlandajo, was engaged in decorating the Chapel at Chiasso Macerelli with frescoes, his son Lorenzo's finer taste led him to employ Botticelli to paint a series of allegorical subjects in a hall on the *piano nobile* of the villa to which he brought his bride. His friend Poliziano, we may be sure, had a share in the composition of the two paintings, which after remaining buried under a coat of whitewash during three hundred years, were discovered on the walls of the Villa Lemmi, in 1873, and removed nine years afterwards to the Louvre.

In the one, the bridegroom, a noble and refined youth, wearing a deep violet robe and a red cap on his long fair locks, is admitted into the circle of the Liberal arts, seven bright haired maidens who, sitting in the shade of a laurel grove, welcome this friend of all the Muses, as Poliziano calls him, with gracious smiles and courteous greeting. Dialectic, the youngest of the group, leads Lorenzo by the hand and presents him to Philosophy, the Queen of all the Sciences, who,

55

throned above the rest and wearing a white veil and robe adorned with golden tongues of flame, bids the youthful stranger welcome. At her feet are her five sisters, each with her own symbol. On the right we see Arithmetic, with a table of figures in her hand ; Grammar, with a scorpion ; and Rhetoric, with a scroll unfolded on her knees. On the left we have Geometry, with a square resting upon her shoulder ; Astronomy, with a globe ; and Music, holding a small organ and tambourine in her hands ; while a curly-headed boy bearing a shield with the Tornabuoni arms stands at Lorenzo's feet.

In Sandro's other fresco, the Graces, three lovely maidens with gliding motion and wistful faces, clad in delicately tinted robes of mauve and white and green, bring their gifts of Chastity, Beauty and Love, under the symbol of single flowers, to the lovely Giovanna, who, standing under a portico, clad in a simple red gown and transparent veil, receives their offering in a white handkerchief. Her regular features and rippling hair are the same as in Ghirlandajo's fresco and Niccolo Fiorentino's medal ; the very pearl necklace round her throat is the same ; but there is a charm in her simple robe and sweet serious face which is altogether lacking in these other representations. The roguish little love who bears the Albizzi coat-of-arms at Giovanna's feet has been half effaced, and the whole fresco is badly damaged. But even in their present ruined condition, torn away, as they have been, from their beautiful surroundings in the fair Tuscan villa, Sandro's compositions have a grace and a freshness which nothing can destroy.

The same tragic fate which attended Giuliano and Simonetta, overtook the wedded pair whose union is celebrated in these frescoes. Giovanna died a few years after her marriage, in giving birth to her third

GIOVANNA TORNABUONI AND THE THREE GRACES (LOUVRE).

child, and in the summer of 1497, when he was only thirty-two, Lorenzo was condemned and put to death with four other leading citizens for conspiring to bring back Piero dei Medici. It was a political crime for which the Piagnone party was to pay dearly, and the untimely fate of this brilliant and popular youth was deplored on all sides. Savonarola vainly recommended him to mercy, and that staunch Piagnone, Luca Landucci, owns that he could not keep back his tears when he saw the young Lorenzo's corpse borne past his house on a bier. Such were the sharp and sudden changes which startled the hearts of the Florentines in those troubled times. Well might the poet sing, " *Di doman non c' è certezza.*"

Another wedding which excited great interest among the friends of the Medici was that of Pier Francesco Bini and Lucrezia, the daughter of the Magnifico's strong supporter Francesco Pucci, which took place in 1487, a year after Lorenzo Tornabuoni's marriage. On this occasion Botticelli was desired to adorn four *cassoni* with scenes from Boccaccio's weird tale of Nastagio degli Onesti, and the spectral huntsman, whose hounds devour his hard-hearted mistress in the Pineta of Ravenna. Sandro himself no doubt designed the composition of these panels, which were executed under his supervision by clever scholars and probably passed as his work. Here and there we seem to recognize his own hand in some face or form, as for instance in the charming figure of Nastagio's bride, who is seen rising in horror from the festive board, at the sudden vision of the hunted lady fleeing before the death-hounds. This romantic scene of the banquet in the pine-forest, was in reality, as Mr. Berenson has lately told us, the work of Ghirlandajo's old pupil, Bartolommeo di Giovanni, who had passed into the rival *bottega* and who probably executed the other panels of the series, with the help of Jacopo del Sellajo.

A large number of similar paintings, dealing with Ovidian myths or mediæval romances, with classical or scriptural stories, were produced in Florence during the last decades of the fifteenth century, and were chiefly executed by Sandro's pupils. Such, for instance, is the *Allegory of Abundance* in the Duc d'Aumale's collection at Chantilly, a life-sized figure evidently imitated by some assistant from the master's own drawing of a woman leading a child, and bearing a cornucopia in her hand, in the Malcolm Collection at the British Museum. Such too were Jacopo del Sellajo's *Story of Orpheus and Eurydice*, a subject plainly suggested by Poliziano's "Orfeo," Bartolommeo di Giovanni's *Jason at Colchis*, and *Battle between the Centaurs and Lapithæ*, and the *Death of Lucretia* in the Pitti, and the *Story of Esther* at Chantilly, by that scholar of Botticelli whom Mr. Berenson has dubbed Amico di Sandro. These panels, most of which were designed for the decoration of *cassoni* and other furniture, are of great interest as showing the close connexion between the humanists and painters of Lorenzo's age, and illustrating the domestic life of contemporary Florentines. And they afford a fresh proof of Sandro's sympathy with the intellectual tendencies of the day, and of the extraordinary popularity which his poetic renderings of these themes had acquired in the eyes of his fellow-citizens.

But, ere long, a change came over the spirit of Botticelli's art. In 1489, Fra Girolamo Savonarola began to preach in the Dominican Church of San Marco, a convent which had always been closely connected with the Medici family. Two years later, after a temporary absence, he came back to Florence at the urgent request of Pico della Mirandola, who

Spooner.

MADONNA AND CHILD WITH ST. JOHN (LOUVRE).

begged Lorenzo to send for him, and began that wonderful course of sermons in the Duomo, which was to stir Florence to its depths. The fiery eloquence of the preacher had a strange fascination for the scholars and painters of the Medici circle. Marsilio Ficino and Poliziano, the poets Girolamo and Benivieni, and the young Michelangelo all heard him gladly. Pico della Mirandola, the Magnifico's dearest friend, and the most brilliant scholar of his day, became one of Fra Girolamo's most devoted followers and died in his arms. Lorenzo himself sent for Savonarola on his death-bed and received his last blessing. The frequent allusions to Plato that we find in Savonarola's sermons, and the bold rebukes which he addressed to painters, show that both scholars and artists were among the crowds which flocked to hear him. And just as the Frate's strong faith in the unseen kindled the interest of the Platonists who belonged to the Medici circle, so the prophetic note in his teaching appealed in a special manner to the mystic side of Sandro's nature ; while the sincerity of the man, his deep human sympathy, could not fail to touch a chord in the painter's breast.

" He became a partisan of the sect of Fra Girolamo," says Vasari in his contemptuous way, " and for this cause abandoned painting. And since he had not money enough to live upon, his affairs soon fell into the greatest disorder. Being obstinately attached to this party he became what was known as a *Piagnone* (a ' sniveller ') and gave up painting, and was reduced to such poverty in his old age that he would have died of hunger, if it had not been for the alms of Lorenzo dei Medici and other friends and men of substance who admired his genius."

There is as usual a germ of truth in Vasari's exaggerated language. Sandro did not give up his art,

neither was he reduced to the point of starvation.
But instead of painting Greek myths and nude god-
desses, he devoted himself almost exclusively to
religious subjects and devotional pictures. The influence of Savonarola's teaching is apparent in many of
his most popular works, more especially in the *tondi*
of the Virgin and Child surrounded with child-angels
which he and his followers repeated in so many
different forms. These sorrowful Madonnas, bur-
dened with a mysterious sentiment of coming anguish,
these fair children whose faces seem to have caught
some mournful foreboding as they gaze on the countenance of Mary, must have been inspired by the
burning words in which the Frate describes the
Mother of Many Sorrows.

In the absence of dates and documents, it is difficult
to speak positively of the order in which Sandro's
well-known Madonnas were painted, and to divide
the pictures that belong to the eighties from those
that were painted in the nineties. It is a question on
which the best critics seldom agree and which must
remain for the present uncertain. The only one of
his altar-pieces to which a date can be positively
assigned is the *Madonna enthroned between St. John
the Baptist and St. John the Evangelist,* now in the
Berlin Museum. This noble work was painted in
1485, for the chapel of the Bardi in Brunellesco's
newly restored church of San Spirito. In a book of
accounts which was lately discovered in the Guic-
ciardini archives by Signor Supino, we find an entry
of the payments made by Giovanni dei Bardi to the
architect and wood-carver Giuliano di San Gallo, on
the 7th of February, for the frame supplied by him
for Sandro del Botticello's altar-piece. Six months
later, there is a second entry from which we learn that
on the 3rd of August Sandro himself received seventy-

Houghton

MADONNA OF THE POMEGRANATE (UFFIZI).

five gold florins : thirty-eight for the gold and wood of the panel, two more for the azure used, and thirty-five for his own work.

The Madonna is enthroned on a richly-carved pedestal of coloured marbles, under a bower of palm, myrtle and cypress, between the venerable white-bearded Evangelist and the noble and ascetic Baptist. The Virgin's face closely resembles that of the goddess in the *Birth of Venus*, which was probably painted immediately after Sandro's return from Rome, and the laughing child, holding out both arms to his mother, is one of the few happy and joyous types of childhood which he has given us. The foliage of the background, the tall white lilies and olive bushes standing in enamelled flower-pots, the red and white roses in the bowls on the marble parapet, are painted with exquisite care, and this combination of natural beauty and artistic ornament produces the finest decorative effect.

Closely related to this work is the large and important altar-piece of the *Madonna and Saints* in the Accademia of Florence, which Sandro painted, probably a year or two later, for the church of S. Barnaba. Here the Virgin is seated on a lofty throne supported by marble columns of rich Renaissance architecture. Two attendant angels draw back the crimson velvet hangings of the canopy, while two others gaze sadly at the instruments of the Passion, the nails and crown of thorns, which they hold up in their hands. The Child, standing on the Virgin's knee, lifts His hand in blessing, and both Mother and Son seem to muse sorrowfully over the mournful tokens of His coming Passion. On the wide marble pavement at the foot of the throne stand six Saints, types of struggling and sanctified humanity. On one side we see the youthful warrior Michael, the aged scholar Saint Augustine, and St. John the prophet of the desert. On the other we have a black-bearded St. Barnabas, St. Ambrose with book and mitre, and the virgin-martyr St. Katharine, robed in blue, with the palm of victory in her hand and a soft expression of heavenly contemplation on her fair features. Both in type and attitude this Saint strongly resembles the reclining goddess in the panel of *Mars and Venus* and the young woman carrying wood in the fresco of the Sistine Chapel. The predella to this picture is also in the Accademia, and consists of a Risen Christ and three little scenes from the lives of the Saints in the altar-piece, the Death of St. Ambrose, St. Augustine's Vision of the Child on the sea-shore, and Salome bearing St. John the Baptist's head on a charger.

The face of the Virgin in the S. Barnaba altar-piece in its sad and meditative expression bears a marked likeness to the *Madonna of the Pomegranate*, that beautiful *tondo* which came to the Uffizi from the collection of the Grand Dukes, and may have once belonged to the Medici. In form and colouring, in the transparent veil which rests on the Madonna's hair, in the lovely faces and curly locks of the six child-angels who press round the Virgin with their blossoming lilies and open choir-books, this *tondo* resembles the *Magnificat*. But here the note of mournful yearning is still more prominent, and the angel faces seem to reflect the tender sadness that is seen on the countenances both of Mother and Child.

Of later date is the *tondo* of the Ambrosiana, in which the kneeling Virgin bends over the Child, supported by an angel, and we catch a charming glimpse of river and woodland beyond the marble parapet, while in the winged seraphs with fluttering draperies and streaming locks, who hold back the curtains of the baldacchino, we have a reminiscence

Houghton.

THE VIRGIN OF THE "MAGNIFICAT" (UFFIZI).

Houghton.

ANGELS FROM THE "MAGNIFICAT" (UFFIZI).

of the St. Barnaba altar-piece. In the Poldi-Pezzoli panel, the Virgin looks down with exquisite tenderness at the unconscious Child on her knee, as He plays with the crown of thorns and nails, while she turns a page of her missal. In the background we have a lovely prospect of park-like landscape, seen through a square casement which recalls the early *Chigi Madonna* and the *Annunciation* which one of Botticelli's assistants painted in 1490, for the Cistercian monks of Cestello. A variation of this composition appears in Mr. Heseltine's little picture, where the St. John kneeling before the Child with a staff in his hand and a halo round his brow, was probably added by a pupil.

But the most famous, the most perfect of all Sandro's Madonnas, is *Our Lady of the Magnificat*. In beauty of design, in lovely transparency of colour, in exquisite finish and depth of feeling, this *tondo* surpasses all Botticelli's other sacred pictures. The way in which the curving lines of meeting hands, interlaced arms and bowed heads all converge, reveals the mastery of design to which Sandro had attained, and the ideal of divine sorrow and tenderness expressed in the Virgin's face remains unsurpassed in the pages of Christian art. At the very moment when she realizes all her glory, when angels place the crown on her brows and the Child guides her hand to write the words that proclaim her blessed among women, the sword pierces her heart with its mysterious foretaste of coming agony.

The wonderful success which Sandro's Madonnas obtained, the amazing demand which sprang up on all sides for these *tondi* of Virgins and angels, was doubtless partly due to the new religious fervour which animated all classes in Florence during the brief period of Savonarola's revival. Every devout *Piagnone*, each pious soul who strove to follow the Frates' rule of holy living, saw in the tender melancholy of Sandro's Madonnas the fulfilment of a cherished ideal. And if the master himself was too much absorbed in mystical dreams and too deeply interested in watching the development of public events to paint with his old industry, the scholars and assistants in his *bottega* made good use of their opportunity. Countless were the *replicas*, endless the imitations which issued from Botticelli's workshops in those days. " Sandro drew exceedingly well," writes Vasari, " so much so that all artists were eager to obtain his drawings." These drawings were reproduced in a hundred different forms. The very slightest of his motives, the roses and the blossoming lilies in his sketches of *Purgatorio* or *Paradiso*, a lighted candle or a spray of olive, were eagerly seized upon and adapted to new and varied uses by his followers. Often they had recourse to some of his earliest designs, such, for instance, as the *Chigi Madonna*, which some clever assistant reproduced in a painting, now at Chantilly, leaving out the symbolic offering of corn and grapes, and substituting a rose and basket of flowers in their stead.

The very men who had repeated Botticelli's Greek myths and classical *fantasie*, ten years before, Jacopo del Sellajo, Bartolommeo di Giovanni, Biagio Tucci, now gave themselves up to the manufacture of Madonnas and Angels. Jacopo's hand has been recognized in the charming *Lichtenstein Madonna*, with the six angels bearing flowering lilies, and Biagio probably painted the Virgin with the eight angels wreathed with roses carrying lighted candles in the Raczynski Collection at Berlin. As for Ghirlandajo's old pupil, Bartolommeo, the painter of *Nastagio degli Onesti's Banquet*, Mr. Berenson tells us that he devoted his whole time to supplying designs for the woodcuts for those small books of " Sacre Rappresen-

THE ANNUNCIATION (SCHOOL WORK).

MADONNA FROM THE "ANNUNCIATION" (A SCHOOL WORK).

tazioni " which were published in Florence during the last decade of the fifteenth century. Several of these are directly connected with Savonarola's life and preaching, and may have been the origin of Vasari's assertion that after his return from Rome, Sandro wasted his time in designing unsuccessful engravings, the best of which was the *Triumph of the Faith of Fra Girolamo*. Then, too, another artist who worked both under Botticelli and Filippino, Raffaellino del Garbo, painted the moving *Pietà* of the Munich Gallery, which is, as it were, a living embodiment of Savonarola's most eloquent and pathetic discourses, and which was, there can be little doubt, designed by Sandro himself.

Two larger works from Botticelli's own hand are believed by many good authorities to belong to this period. One is the *Coronation of the Virgin* in the Accademia, which was ordered by the Guild of Silk-weavers for Savonarola's own convent-church of S. Marco. The upper part of this altar-piece is painted on a gold ground, like Fra Angelico's works, which in some respects it resembles. Both the venerable figure of God the Father in the triple crown and the bending form of the Holy Virgin follow the traditional type ; but no one excepting Sandro could have invented the troop of angels who, dancing hand in hand in a tumult of wild rapture, scattering roses on the clouds in their circling flight, while one blue-robed seraph borne heavenward by irresistible might of love, darts up to Mary's side, and seems to claim a share in her joy and triumph. In the green meadow below, four Saints contemplate the vision that has dawned on their wondering sight : St. Jerome in his cardinal's hat, St. Augustine and St. Eligius, rapt in studious medita-tion, and St. John the Evangelist, with his arm uplifted and eyes turned heavenwards in a passion of love and yearning. The vehement action of this aged

E

Saint and the rapid flight of the angel-children seem to indicate that this Coronation belongs to the time when Savonarola's influence had already affected Sandro's art, and the serenity of his earlier conceptions had given place to more passionate and emotional feelings. It was probably painted early in the nineties. Dr. Julius Meyer, indeed, places this altar-piece as late as 1497, and Signor Supino thinks that the dancing angels may have been suggested by the white-robed children who danced round the Sacrifice of Vanities on the Piazza. Mr. Berenson, on the contrary, believes it to have been painted as early as 1480.

The Predella of this Coronation, consisting of an Annunciation, with a blue-robed Virgin seated in her chamber, and four scenes from the lives of the Saints represented above. St. Augustine is seen writing in his cell, St. John meditating in the Isle of Patmos, St. Jerome kneels before a crucifix, and St. Eligius is shoeing a horse which is led by the devil in the form of a fair young woman wearing a green robe, while his horns peep out from under her flowing locks.

The same vehement gestures, the same sense of strong emotion, are seen in a still greater degree in the unfinished picture which was brought to the Uffizi from the Palazzo Vecchio early in the last century, and is probably the *Adoration of the Magi* mentioned by the Anonimo Gaddiano as having been painted by Sandro at the top of a staircase in the Palazzo leading to the door of the Catena. Botticelli's hand is clearly recognized in the composition, which bears a strong resemblance to Leonardo's unfinished *Adoration* in the Uffizi. Unfortunately Sandro only sketched the picture in *tempera*, and, more than a hundred years afterwards, the whole of the panel was coarsely repainted in oils by some inferior artist. The scene is laid in a wide, mountainous landscape, where

66

Houghton.

CORONATION OF THE VIRGIN, (ACCADEMIA. FLORENCE).

Houghton.

DANCING ANGELS FROM THE "CORONATION"
(ACCADEMIA, FLORENCE).

the Holy Family are seated in a rocky cavern under precipitous cliffs, which recall the background of *Pallas and the Centaur*. In the foreground are eight kneeling figures, who may be intended to represent the chief magistrates of Florence (the *Otto*), since they bring no offerings in their hands and wear no badge of kingly rank. Through the clefts in the rocks we see the vast concourse of people of all classes eagerly streaming in through the city gates to take part in the same great act of worship. Young and old men and women are stirred by the same feverish excitement, the same tumultuous emotion. Some clasp both hands together in earnest supplication, others point with outstretched arms to the Child-Christ on His mother's knee. One leader on horseback lifts his right hand with commanding gesture, summoning his men to follow ; another shades his eyes from the blaze of light which the bright beams of the Star throws over the Holy Child. Many portraits have been recognized among the foremost figures. On the right is Girolamo Benivieni, the poet who gave up writing carnival songs to compose hymns and carols for the children of San Marco. Behind him stands a tall figure in a flowing robe and long white beard, resting his chin meditatively on his hand, who bears a marked resemblance to Sandro's old friend Leonardo. On the left, behind St. Joseph, a Dominican friar, probably intended for Savonarola himself, points with fervent devotion to the new-born King, and turning to a grey-haired figure, in whom some critics recognize Lorenzo dei Medici, at his side, adjures him to own the supremacy of Christ. This *Adoration*, which differs in so many respects from Sandro's other versions of the subject, was evidently intended to commemorate the crowning triumph of the Frate's revival, when after the expulsion of Piero dei Medici and the departure of the French army, a popular form of government was drawn up and Christ was proclaimed King in Florence. The scene may have been suggested to Sandro by an event which took place at the Feast of Epiphany in 1498, when the Signory of Florence went in state to San Marco and paid their offerings to the Prior, whose hand they kissed as he stood before the altar.

This unfinished painting may possibly be that memorable representation of the *Triumph of the Faith of Fra Girolamo*, which Vasari tells us was the subject of Sandro's best and finest engraving. When only a few months afterwards, the great revival which was to have made Florence the City of God had closed in tears and gloom and Savonarola and his companions had died at the stake, Botticelli's picture was naturally put aside and only brought out again to be painted over by some inferior artist in the next century. Such at least is the interpretation of this picture which, originally suggested by Signor Milanesi and Mr. Heath Wilson on its discovery in 1881, has been accepted by Dr. Ulmann, Signor Venturi, M. Eugène Muntz, Signor Supino, and other well-known critics. Mr. Horne, however, dismisses the idea as absurd, and is of opinion that the work belongs to a much earlier period and was painted before Sandro's visit to Rome.

MADONNA WITH ANGELS BEARING TAPERS (BERLIN).

V

1492—1510

AS long as Lorenzo dei Medici lived, he was a good friend to Botticelli. On the 4th January, 1491, the painter was appointed member of a commission which met to choose a design for the façade of the Duomo, and on the 18th of May he was chosen, together with the two Ghirlandajo brothers, and the miniaturists Gherardo and Monte di Giovanni, to execute mosaics for the chapel of St. Zenobius in the same church. But the work was interrupted by the death of the Magnifico at Careggi on the 8th of April, 1492. In him Florence lost the greatest of her rulers, and her artists were deprived of their most enlightened patron.

Botticelli never seems to have entertained any relations with Lorenzo's unworthy son Piero, who soon disgusted his father's best friends by his violence and folly ; but he still clung to his old patron, Lorenzo di Pier Francesco. Fortunately for artists, this cousin of the Magnifico, as well as his younger brother Giovanni, had both joined the popular party, and were allowed to remain in Florence during the political changes that followed on the great Lorenzo's death. It was probably about this time that Sandro began his series of drawings on the " Divina Commedia " for this patron, and when, on the 14th of July, 1496, young Michelangelo wrote from Rome to Lorenzo di

Pier Francesco, who had sent him with introductions to his friends in that city, he addressed his letter to Sandro Botticelli in a cover bearing the characteristic *Piagnone* inscription—" *Christus* " !

Two years later, in 1498, the year of Savonarola's execution, we learn from a new income-tax return, that Sandro was still living in his old home in the Via Nuova. Both his father and elder brother Giovanni were dead, and the house was now the property of his nephews, Benincasa and Lorenzo Filipepi. His brother Simone had returned from Naples soon after old Mariano's death at the close of 1493, and also lived under the same roof and shared a country-house (*Casa di Signore*) in the parish of San Sepolcro, outside the gate of San Frediano, with Sandro. The brothers, it appears, had bought this house, together with an old vineyard and some fields, in April 1494, for the sum of 156 florins, as well as a yearly quit-rent of 4 soldi and a pair of capons, which they paid to the Hospital of Santa Maria Nuova.

Simone Filipepi seems to have been a cultivated man, who shared his brother's love of Dante, and wrote a commentary on a canzone by the poet of the " Divina Commedia." Like Sandro, he was an ardent *Piagnone*, and the Chronicle in which he recorded contemporary events is a proof of his intimate connexion with the Friar's party and of his personal attachment to Savonarola. Every incident in the great revival is here faithfully described. Sandro himself must have told his brother of that prophetic sermon in which the Frate, one April evening in 1492, foretold the coming troubles—" *Ecce gladius Domini . . . super terram cito et velociter.*" That same night, Simone writes in his journal, the cupola of the Duomo was struck with lightning, and three days afterwards Lorenzo il Magnifico died at Careggi. The writer

CALUMNY (UFFIZI).

dwells with delight on the wonderful fervour and religious enthusiasm which stirred the whole city, on the thousands who flocked to the Duomo, and the crowds that waited for hours at the doors to see the Frate pass. He describes the marvellous effect of Savonarola's sermons—" When he mounted the pulpit steps, he was a new St. Paul," and recalls the happy summer evenings when they walked with the friars and novices in the quiet gardens of San Marco, and heard the Frate expound the Gospel in simple words. " Then, indeed, for an hour or two, one seemed to be in Paradise, so great was the devotion and simplicity shown by all, and blessed were those who were present at these gatherings." With the same vivid touches, Sandro's brother narrates the horror of the last struggle, the midnight attack on the convent, the mock trial, the terrible tale of torture and prison, and the final scene of the execution on the Piazza, which he witnessed with his own eyes. Darker still is the picture which he paints of the days of persecution which followed, when all fear of God and reverence for holy things had died out, when blasphemy and sacrilege went unpunished, and " hell itself seemed to open, and all the devils were let loose." Then the vilest calumnies were heaped on the Frate and his followers, and no one could speak his name without peril to his life. Simone fled for safety to Bologna, but Sandro remained in Florence. His old connexion with the Medici and the friendship of Lorenzo di Pier Francesco stood him in good stead ; but he saw the crime and misery about him, and shared in the deep dejection of the faithful *Piagnoni*, who had believed in the prophet's word, and looked for the coming of the New Jerusalem that was to be set up on earth.

Then it was that, in the bitterness of his soul, Sandro painted his *Allegory of Calumny*, and gave it

71

to his dearest and most intimate friend, Antonio Segni,
the same for whom Leonardo made his noble drawing
of *Neptune and the Sea-gods*. The subject was taken
from Lucian's "Dialogues," and had become familiar
to Florentine artists from the version which was given
by Alberti in his "Treatise on Painting." The scene
is laid in a stately columned portico adorned with
antique statues and bas-reliefs in chiaroscuro height-
ened with gold. Old Greek myths are mingled
with Bible stories in the subjects here represented.
Pallas, with the Gorgon's head appears by the side of
Judith and Holofernes and St. George and the Dragon.
Apollo and Daphne, the Battle of the Centaurs,
Venus and Amorini, Trajan and the Widow are
introduced, together with statues of prophets and
apostles and a single figure of St. George, which
recalls at once Donatello's warrior in the niche of
Or San Michele, and Andrea del Castagno's portrait
of Pippo Spano. In this noble Renaissance hall a
fearful crime is being perpetrated in the name of
Justice. The unjust judge, clad in a green robe,
bearing a crown and sceptre, is seated on his throne,
while Ignorance and Suspicion whisper malicious
accusations into his "long ears." Envy, a pale and
squalid figure, clad in shaggy skins, reaches out a
skinny hand to arrest the judge's attention, and leads
forward Calumny, a richly-dressed woman bearing a
lighted torch, who drags prostrate Innocence by the
hair along the floor. Her attendants, Fraud and
Treachery, wait upon her footsteps and wreath roses
in her hair, while the boy Innocence lifts his clasped
hands to invoke the help of God. At his feet stands
Remorse, an old hag, wearing a black mantle over
her ragged clothes, and leaning on a crutch as she
looks back over her shoulder at the nude form of the
golden-haired maiden Truth, who, fair as the Venus

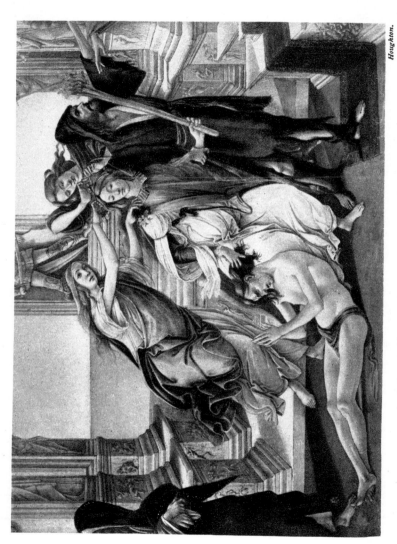

CALUMNY AND INNOCENCE (DETAIL). (UFFIZI).

Anadyomene of old, is seen lifting her hand to heaven
in the calm certainty that there her mute appeal will
be heard. Through the open arches of the loggia we
look out on a wide waste of green waters and distant
horizon, which leave an indefinite sense of dreariness
on the mind—the expression of the painter's conviction that Truth and Justice were nowhere to be
found on earth. This allegory, in which the classical
ideals of his early manhood are combined with the
bitter experiences of later years, was Sandro's silent
protest against the tragedy of Savonarola's end.
When he painted that inspired vision of Truth, who
can doubt that he remembered the burning words in
which the Frate ended his great course of sermons on
the psalm, *Quam bonus*—" Wine is strong, the king is
strong, women are stronger, but Truth is mightier
than all, and will prevail ? "

Even in these dark days Sandro's faith in the Friar
never faltered. Every line of Simone's chronicle
breathes the same profound conviction that this man
whom Florence had rejected and put to death was a
prophet sent from God. The writer notes how one
by one the words of Fra Girolamo have come true,
and dwells with satisfaction on the violent and
miserable end which had overtaken all his enemies—
Pope Alexander VI, Cæsar Borgia, King Alfonso of
Naples, Lodovico Sforza and many more. And he
records the unwilling testimony borne to Savonarola's
innocence and saintliness by his jailors and persecutors,
most of all by Doffo Spini, the riotous captain of the
Compagnacci who led the attack on San Marco, and
was present at the Frate's trial.

In the *Giornale* of Lorenzo Violi, the young notary
who wrote down all Savonarola's sermons, we find
repeated allusions to the " Academy of unemployed
artists," who met in these days in Sandro Botticelli's

workshop and disputed much about the Friar. Simone, the writer tells us, was often present on these occasions, and wrote down some of these discussions in his chronicle. Amongst others, Simone records the following conversation which took place on the Feast of All Souls, being the 2nd November, 1499 :—

"Alessandro di Mariano, my brother, one of the good painters which our city had in these times, being at home, by the fire, about eight o'clock at night, related how that day, in his shop in the house of Sandro, he had reasoned with Doffo Spini on the fate of Fra Girolamo. Sandro, knowing Doffo to have been one of the chief persons who were present at his examination, adjured him to tell him truthfully what crimes were found in him which could deserve so shameful a death. Upon which Doffo replied, 'Sandro, must I speak the truth? We never found in him any venial, much less any mortal sin.' Then Sandro asked, 'Why did you put him to so shameful a death?' He replied, 'It was not I, but Benozzo Federighi. For, if we had not made this prophet and his companions die, and had sent them back to San Marco, the people would have sacked our houses and cut us all to pieces.'"

This interesting record throws light on the picture of the *Nativity*, which Sandro painted a few months after that November evening when he extorted Doffo Spini's confession of Fra Girolamo's innocence. It is clearly one of those works which, like the medals and portraits of Savonarola and the paintings of his execution, were handed down among the hidden treasures of some Piagnone family of Florence during centuries. Sixty years ago it was brought to England by Mr. Young Ottley, and in 1878, passed from the Fuller-Maitland Collection into the National Gallery. This time the story of the Birth of Christ is trans-

THE NATIVITY (NATIONAL GALLERY).

formed by the painter's soaring fancy into a mystic vision of the Triumph of Savonarola and the fulfilment of his word. The Holy Family as usual form the central group, and the rude wooden penthouse is set in a rocky cavern in the heart of a pine forest. On the right a winged angel, with an olive branch in his hand, brings the shepherds to the stable of Bethlehem ; on the left another seraph points out the Child to the kneeling kings from the Far East. Three angels, clad in symbolic hues of red, white and green, and bearing olive branches in their hands, sing the *Gloria in Excelsis* on the penthouse roof, and in the blue sky above, twelve more seraphs dance hand-in-hand, swinging their olive boughs to and fro, and dangling their golden crowns in a wild ecstasy of triumphant joy.

The hour, long foretold by the Cumæan Sibyl on the banks of Lake Avernus, has come at length and there is joy in heaven, peace and goodwill on earth. The Virgin's face has lost all trace of care and sadness, and the Child laughs with joy as He looks up in His mother's face. In the foreground devils are seen hurrying away to hide among the rocks, while rejoicing angels fall on the necks of Fra Girolamo and his martyred companions, and welcome them with rapturous embraces. In order that there should be no doubt as to the identity of the three saints crowned with olive and wearing the Dominican habit, with the witnesses slain for the word of their testimony as told in the Revelation of St. John, Sandro has placed the following inscription in Greek letters on the upper part of his panel :—"This picture I, Alessandro, painted at the end of the year 1500, during the troubles of Italy in the half-time after the time which was prophesied in the Eleventh of St. John and the Second Woe of the Apocalypse, when the devil was loosed upon the earth for three years and a half. Afterwards he shall be put in chains according to the Twelfth, and we shall see him trodden under foot as in this picture." So the painter would have us know that, in these dark and desperate times, his faith in the Friar had never failed, and that he still looked forward to a day when the prophet's word should be fulfilled and good triumph over evil.

A pen drawing for the central group of this picture —the tall form of the kneeling Madonna and the St. Joseph crouching behind the Child—is still preserved among a few of the painter's studies in the Uffizi. Both in the faulty proportions of these figures, in the hasty execution of the face, we see evident signs of decay and advancing years ; but the colour of the picture is rich and glowing, and the dancing angels are as light and joyous in their movement as any which Sandro drew of old. Above all, the artist's imagination is as full of fire and buoyancy, his faith and love are as strong as in the youthful days when he first worked for the Medici.

Botticelli lived ten years after he finished this *Nativity*. Whether he painted other pictures remains uncertain, but several small works belong to his later years, and were probably executed towards the close of the century. To this period Morelli ascribes the little picture of *St. Augustine*, who is here represented writing under an arched recess adorned with medallions touched with gold, similar to the bas-relief in the *Calumny*. This work, which is now in the Uffizi (No. 1179), is one of those "most beautiful little paintings" by Sandro which are mentioned by Antonio Billi and the Anonimo Gaddiano. These writers also allude to another "work of rare beauty," a little *St. Jerome*, which some critics identify with a small picture of St. Jerome receiving his last com-

MADONNA DI S. BARNABA (ACCADEMIA, FLORENCE).

munion under a rude hut that is still the property of the Marchese Farinola in Florence.

To these closing years of the master's life we may ascribe with greater certainty two very interesting works, the *Story of Virginia* in the Morelli Gallery at Bergamo, and the *Death of Lucretia* in Mrs. J. L. Gardner's Collection at Boston, in the United States. These long, narrow panels were evidently intended for the decoration of *cassoni* or other furniture, and may belong to the series which Botticelli painted for his old patrons the Vespucci, and which Vasari describes as " full of beautiful and animated figures." Both pictures are remarkable for the imposing character of the classical architecture introduced in the background, as well as for the dramatic power with which the different incidents in those tragic stories are represented. The Bergamo panel has the additional advantage of being in excellent preservation, and retains much of its original richness and harmony of colour.

Closely related to these Roman subjects are the panels on the *Life and Miracles of St. Zenobius*. Two of these, in which the baptism and consecration of the good Bishop and his first miracle are represented, now belong to Mr. Ludwig Mond. A third, in which the Saint restores to life a child who has been run over by the wheel of a cart, and gives his last blessing to the priests and people on his deathbed, is in the Dresden Gallery. All of these are marked by the same rich and varied architecture and animated action, but their artistic effect is somewhat marred by the violence of the gestures and by the extravagant display of emotion in the leading personages.

These last designs were probably intended for the decoration of the Chapel of St. Zenobius in the Duomo, a work which, after being abandoned for many years, was at length resumed, early in 1504, by the Gonfalionere Piero Soderini, a brother of Sandro's old friend Tommaso. They certainly belong to the painter's declining years, and betray evident marks of advancing age and failing power.

Another interesting little picture of this period, in which Mr. Berenson and other critics of authority have recognized the master's hand, is the so-called *Derelitta* or *Outcast* in the Pallavicini Palace in Rome. A young woman in a ragged white linen garment is seen weeping bitterly on the steps of a Renaissance palace. Her long, dark hair falls over her face, her head is buried in her hands, and her other clothes lie strewn on the stone steps. In her silence and loneliness she is the very image of inconsolable despair. There is some resemblance to the garments worn by Remorse in the picture of *Calumny*, but it is difficult to believe that this work, which is so curiously modern in style and sentiment, should have been painted by a fifteenth century artist.

But the great work to which Sandro devoted the last years of his life was the illustration of Dante's " Divina Commedia." From the first, Botticelli had shared the revived enthusiasm for Dante which distinguished the humanists of the Medici circle. He was, we know, an ardent student of the " Divina Commedia," and a line from the Paradiso, " *Vergine madre, figlia del tuo figlio*," is inscribed on the steps of the throne in the altar-piece of the *Madonna and Saints* which he painted for the Church of S. Barnaba. There is little doubt that he designed the nineteen plates for the edition by the German printer Nicolaus Lorenz, or Nicolo della Magna, as the Italians called him, with Cristoforo Landino's commentary, which was published at Florence in 1481. In later years he illustrated a volume of Dante on parchment sheets for

MADONNA AND CHILD (POLDI-PEZZOLI, MILAN).

his old friend Lorenzo di Pier Francesco, a work which the Anonimo tells us " was held to be a marvellous thing."

It was this illustrated " Dante " which Dr. Waagen discovered fifty years ago among the treasures of Hamilton Palace, and in which he immediately recognized the hand of Botticelli. In 1882, this precious volume was purchased by the Prussian Government at the Hamilton sale, and is now the property of the Berlin Museum. Besides the eighty-five drawings at Berlin, eight others, including a coloured plan of the Inferno, were recently discovered by Dr. Strzygowsky, in a volume which formerly belonged to Queen Christina of Sweden and is now in the Vatican Library. These had evidently formerly belonged to the original volume in the Hamilton Collection, and must have been removed in the seventeenth century. Eight others, belonging to the early cantos of the " Inferno," are still missing.

The whole series originally consisted of a hundred drawings, as well as the title-page and diagram of Hell. All of these were originally drawn with a soft silver-point supposed to contain an alloy of lead, and afterwards roughly traced over with pen and ink. Only three of them are painted in body colour, while a fourth, illustrating Canto x., in the Vatican, is partly tinted, the figure of Dante being painted red, and that of Virgil blue. Many of the drawings are badly damaged and half effaced, while as compositions they are of very unequal merit. But in spite of these defects, the whole series is of the deepest interest, and deserves to rank among the finest and most imaginative works of the Renaissance. To this day Sandro's illustrations remain the best and most satisfying artistic interpretation of Dante's great epic that has ever been attempted, and every page proves how

79

deeply and truly the painter had entered into the poet's meaning.

The master's hand is plainly visible throughout. We recognize his peculiar type of features, the wistful expression of his faces, his skill in depicting rapid movement and flying draperies. We see his love of natural beauty in the delicate drawing of foliage and plants, in the orange and myrtle, the palms and pomegranates of the " *divina foresta spessa e viva,*" where Matilda plucks flowers in the grassy meadows on the banks of the river Eunoë, and Dante's eyes are at length gladdened by the sight of Beatrice.

The artist's evident anxiety to keep closely to the text of the poem and his adoption of mediæval imagery have not, it is true, always proved successful. But if some of the illustrations of the " Inferno " appear crowded and confused, others again are full of grandeur and originality. Such for instance is the illustration of Canto xxxi, where the six Giants are represented bound in chains on the brink of the nethermost pit, and Antæus bends down to lower Dante and Virgil into the abyss below. Here the admirable foreshortening and fine modelling of the nude forms recall Pollaiuolo's style and remind us of Sandro's early studies under this master. But it is in the latter cantos of the " Purgatorio " and in the " Paradiso," that the mystic poetry of Botticelli's imagination finds free play. The vision of his Lady, " *si bella e ridente,*" throned on the car of the Church, attended by dancing Angels and Virtues, and Elders bearing the open books of the Gospels in their hands ; the upward flight of Beatrice and the poet through the wind-blown trees, and the different scenes in which his adored mistress is seen, with lifted hand and serious air, expounding the mysteries of the Faith to the listening poet, are all conceived in Sandro's happiest manner. Many of his favourite motives, the single roses fluttering through the air, the angels bearing lighted candlesticks and olive branches, are introduced in these latter subjects. And when in the 28th Canto we reach the higher spheres of Heaven, and the poet gazes with dazzled eyes on the nine orders of seraphim, Beatrice herself appears under the familiar form of Spring, with the same rippling hair and the same radiant smile, immortal in her youth and loveliness. Here, on the left of the central group, in the lowest tier of angels, we discover one little cherub holding a *cartellino* in his hand, on which we read the artist's name—Sandro di Mariano. Perhaps in these words, written in the same minute characters as the lines from Dante which are inscribed along the margin of these drawings, we may read an expression of the master's pious hope that his soul might at the last be numbered among the elect, and share in the bliss of Heaven.

Lorenzo di Pier Francesco, the patron for whom the work was originally intended, died in 1503, probably before Sandro had finished his book of drawings, but in all likelihood the painter continued to work at the series for some years after this. Several of the leaves intended to illustrate the concluding cantos of " Paradiso " have, however, been left blank. Only the last drawing, which was to represent the Rose of Heaven, is sketched in, and the figures of Christ and His Mother with the Archangel Gabriel flying upwards, are slightly indicated, as if the pen had dropped from the master's hand before the work was complete.

On the 25th January, 1504, Botticelli was summoned, with all the leading artists in Florence, to choose a site for Michelangelo's colossal statue of David. His old friends Leonardo da Vinci, and the architect

Giuliano di San Gallo, the painter Cosimo Rosselli who had worked with him in the Sistine Chapel, his pupil Filippino Lippi, the Piagnone architect Cronaca, and Giovanni delle Corniole, who carved the portrait of Savonarola on a well-known gem, Piero di Cosimo and Baccio d'Agnolo were all present at the meeting, which took place in the Opera del Duomo. On this occasion Sandro supported Cosimo Rosselli's suggestion that the giant ought to stand in front of the Duomo in the following words : " Cosimo has said where in my opinion the statue ought to be placed, to be seen by the passers-by, by the side of Judith, on the steps of Santa Maria del Fiore, or else in the Loggia dei Signori, but rather at the corner of the church, and this I judge to be the best place." Giuliano di San Gallo and Leonardo, on the contrary, were strongly in favour of placing the statue in the Loggia, fearing the effect that exposure to weather would have on the marble, while Filippino and Piero di Cosimo proposed that the choice of the spot should be left to Michelangelo himself, " as he will know better than us how it should be." This last resolution was unanimously accepted, and by the sculptor's wish the great statue was set up on the steps of the Palazzo.

After this we hear no more of Sandro. All we have is Vasari's melancholy picture of the old painter, infirm and helpless, unable to stand upright and supporting himself with two crutches. At length, on the 17th of May, 1510, death came to his release, and he was buried with his fathers in the vault of Ognissanti, his parish church.

The great popularity which Botticelli had enjoyed during his lifetime did not long survive his death. The influence of new aims and ideals ; above all, the passion to emulate Michelangelo's grand style, which swept like a wave over Florentine art in the early years

of the sixteenth century, all contributed to wipe out
the memory of the past, and before longthe very
name of Botticelli was forgotten. When, a hundred
years after his death, the Grand Duke Ferdinand, a
member of the younger branch of the house of Medici,
issued a decree to prohibit the removal of works of
art from the churches of Florence, only two painters
belonging to the fifteenth century, Filippino and
Perugino, were included in the list, and Botticelli's
name was not even mentioned. During the next four
hundred years his fame remained buried in oblivion,
and it was only towards the close of the nineteenth
century that the high artistic excellence and rare
genius of this great master were once more fully
recognized and appreciated.